Advance Praise for *Financial Fitness Forever*

"Investors need smart, reliable advice more than ever. Paul Merriman lays out a ground plan that combines deep understanding of the markets with sober common sense. An essential guide."

—Henry K. "Bud" Hebeler, retired president,
Boeing Aerospace Co., and founder,
www.analyzenow.com

"We have long relied on Paul Merriman's expert financial advice. If you buy only one new book on how to manage your investments, make it this one."

—Martin Edelston, chairman,
Bottom Line Publications

"Paul Merriman reveals the strategies that have helped so many of his clients achieve financial security. He combines top technical knowledge with a deep understanding of the human side of investing."

—James Lange, author,
Retire Secure

"Peace of mind and trust are at a premium in these uncertain financial times. Paul Merriman shows you how to find both and use them to create a personal financial plan that gets results you probably didn't think were possible."

—Ed Slott, CPA, and founder,
IRAhelp.com

FINANCIAL
FITNESS
FOREVER

FINANCIAL FITNESS FOREVER

5 Steps to More Money, Less Risk, and More Peace of Mind

PAUL A. MERRIMAN
WITH RICHARD BUCK

New York Chicago San Francisco Lisbon London Madrid Mexico City
Milan New Delhi San Juan Seoul Singapore Sydney Toronto

1 2 3 4 5 6 7 8 9 10 11 12 13 14 15   QFR/QFR   1 9 8 7 6 5 4 3 2 1

ISBN   978-0-07-178698-0
MHID   0-07-178698-8

e-ISBN 978-0-07-178699-7
e-MHID   0-07-178699-6

This publication is designed to provide accurate and authoritative information in
regard to the subject matter covered. It is sold with the understanding that neither
the author nor the publisher is engaged in rendering legal, accounting, securities
trading, or other professional services. If legal advice or other expert assistance is
required, the services of a competent professional person should be sought.
  —*From a Declaration of Principles Jointly Adopted by a Committee of the American
Bar Association and a Committee of Publishers and Associations*

Library of Congress Cataloging-in-Publication Data

Merriman, Paul A., 1943–
      Financial fitness forever : 5 steps to more money, less risk, and more peace
of mind / by Paul Merriman and Richard Buck.
          p.   cm.
      ISBN-13: 978-0-07-178698-0 (alk. paper)
      ISBN-10: 0-07-178698-8 (alk. paper)
      1. Finance, Personal.   2. Investments.   3. Financial security.
      4. Retirement income—Planning.   I. Buck, Richard, 1944–   II. Title.

      HG179.M4319   2012
      332.024'01—dc23   2011040337

McGraw-Hill books are available at special quantity discounts to use as premiums
and sales promotions or for use in corporate training programs. To contact a
representative, please e-mail us at bulksales@mcgraw-hill.com.

This book is printed on acid-free paper.

I dedicate this book to the women in my life:
my wife, Suzanne;
my daughters, Julie, Larisa, and Lexi;
and my mother, Sarah.

CONTENTS

FOREWORD

Paul Merriman is one really smart guy, but more than that, he is wise. And in investment counseling, I'll take wise over smart any day.

It has been my pleasure to be a guest on his radio program many times over the years, and I have always been struck by the calm, intelligent advice he offers his listeners, just as he does his investment clients. I wouldn't agree to be his guest if I were at all uneasy about the advice he gives, so it's not surprising that his advice conforms very closely to ours in *Kiplinger's Personal Finance* magazine and *Kiplinger's Retirement Report*.

Now, in this superb blueprint for achieving financial security, Paul lays out an orderly path that anyone can follow, with results that, I believe, will be very rewarding. It builds upon his excellent 2008 book, *Live It Up Without Outliving Your Money!*

To get your attention, Paul starts this book with a truly depressing overview of the state of most Americans' retirement situation today—the demise of traditional pensions, woeful undersaving and overconsumption by most Americans, and profligacy by all levels of government, too, which may lead to higher taxes and lower future benefits.

The situation is pretty grim, but don't stop reading. As Paul points out, "We are the ones responsible for our own financial security," and that's both a problem and an exciting opportunity. The chapters that ensue show you how you can take advantage of powerful tools at your disposal: an array of tax-deferred retirement saving devices, academic research on which kind of investments will meet your needs and which won't, and new ways to put your investments on autopilot.

Investors are sometimes their own worst enemies, letting their hearts overrule their heads, running with the herd, and getting caught up in the latest investment mania, like dot-com stocks and IPOs in the late '90s and zero-down-payment homes and condos in the housing bubble of the mid-2000s. Paul is an astute student of investor psychology, and he knows that the best way to keep a cool head when others are losing theirs is to have a sensible plan and stick to it, through markets good and bad. As in sports, disciplined adherence to the game plan is a lot better than panicky, rapid course corrections.

But how do you create a game plan that's right for you? Well, it starts with an allocation of your retirement savings over an array of assets, in a mix that's right for your present age, income, tolerance for risk, retirement expectations, and other sources of retirement income that might be coming your way. A financial planner can help you set an asset allocation formula that's right for you, and you'll find good advice in this book and similar guides.

Too many investors get hung up on having to own the right stocks or investing with the latest hot mutual fund manager. But history shows that investing success is based more on owning the right *mix* of assets than on owning any particular stock or fund. That's because, at any moment in economic history, some broad category of assets—whether U.S. stocks, foreign stocks, bonds, real estate, commodities—will be basking in the sunshine while others languish in the doghouse. But a year or two later, the situation will be very different, and a once-shunned asset class will be the new star. That's why you need to own an array of different kinds of assets, in proportions appropriate to your stage of life.

It's easy just to say you've got to diversify your holdings, but Paul offers specific ideas on how to do it, including some low-cost index mutual funds with built-in diversification and rebalancing to maintain the right mix. You need stocks of companies in these major categories: large multinational firms, both U.S. and foreign (basically, the S&P 500 Index plus a global index like EAFE); smaller companies, both U.S. and foreign, with good growth potential at a fair present price (so-called "value" stocks); and real estate investment trusts (REITs) that own a variety of commercial properties from apartments and office buildings to malls and warehouses.

And that's just the equity component of your portfolio, to which you will need to add bond mutual funds (corporate, Treasury, and municipal bonds) and a component of cash. Some advisers might add a small dollop of commodities through a mutual fund, to benefit from the long trend of rising world prices in energy and food.

Smart asset allocation—spreading your wealth across numerous asset classes—would have saved you from a lot of pain in the brutal bear stock market of 2008–2009. Going in, you'd have owned a lot of bonds (maybe 40 percent or more), which would have cushioned some of your stock declines. And as stocks fell, rebalancing to maintain their assigned share in the mix would have caused you to buy more, even as other investors were fleeing the market. Autopilot rebalancing forces investors to do what's hardest for them: buying low and selling high.

While steering you toward sensible investments, Paul has the courage to name a few investments that virtually nobody needs to own. And he closes one chapter by naming an investor who stands a good chance of outperforming the legendary Warren Buffett in the years ahead. (I won't give away the identity of this person, so you can be surprised.)

Paul Merriman is passionate about providing real help for real people, and that is reflected in a unique feature of this book. In the appendixes is a list of Paul's specific recommendations for the best ways to take advantage of the investment options in 50 of the largest 401(k) retirement plans, including the U.S. Government's Thrift Savings Plan. I have not seen this information anywhere else, and it should be very useful to people trying to make the most of their retirement savings.

Paul has spent a lifetime learning the techniques that make him an outstanding teacher of investing. Now it's your turn to benefit from his knowledge. Make the most of it.

—Knight Kiplinger
Editor in Chief, *The Kiplinger Letter,*
Kiplinger's Personal Finance magazine, and Kiplinger.com

ACKNOWLEDGMENTS

Fortunately, at the age of 68, I am not saddled with financial debts. Even more fortunately, I am deeply indebted to many people who have contributed to my life, to my career, and, of course, to this book.

Bob Marty and Ellyne Lonergan, co-producers of "Financial Fitness After 50" on PBS, helped me evolve my teaching style from numbers-based workshops to a whole new world of television communication. Even better, they did this in a way that made me think the transformation was all my idea. They are great professionals.

Every one of the financial advisors at Merriman Inc. made this a better book by contributing the wisdom they gained from working with thousands of investors. In more ways and more times than I can even remember, they have helped me. They listen to me, encourage me, challenge me, and give me important information that I might not have otherwise.

Phuc Dang generously contributed his tax expertise and reviewed the numbers in Chapter 10 to make sure they were at least in the ballpark of reality. Paresh Kamdar, Mark Metcalf, and Elaine Scoggins reviewed chapter drafts and gave me valuable feedback. Lowell Lombardi Parker spent hours compiling the retirement plan recommendations in the back of the book.

Jeremy Burger and Tyler Bartlett are tireless in their pursuit of the best solutions for investors. I am also very blessed to be able to work with Cheryl Curran, Aaron Spencer, and Eric Jonson, who set extremely high standards in taking care of investors "in the trenches."

Larry Katz, Merriman research director, provided much of the number-crunching in these pages. My wife, Suzanne, showed immense patience and generosity in letting me take on this major project despite my promise that I would slow down. My son and colleague, Jeff Merriman-Cohen, has never wavered in his support and encouragement. Susan Pelton read the final manuscript and gave valuable feedback that I appreciate a lot.

Sam Fleishman, my agent in New York, spent many hours to make sure this book actually got published.

If I had had to create this book by myself, it would have contained something like 150 pages of numbers and 50 pages of text. Fortunately for me, and for my readers too, I have the help of Richard Buck. For nearly 20 years he has added his own experience and ideas to mine and then expressed it all in a clear, concise, and interesting way that I cannot duplicate.

Finally, through the years I have worked and spoken with thousands of investors. I've learned from them all, and every part of this book reflects the things they have taught me.

INTRODUCTION

Nearly half a century ago, as a novice investor, I believed I had discovered how easy it was to make big money in a hurry. I was thrilled. But perhaps I should not have been quite so elated. You'll find the rest of that story, "The Worst Investment I Ever Made," in Chapter 9, "The Worst."

In one way, that may have been the *best* investment I ever made because of what I learned from it. A few years later, after I had been in the securities business a while, I began to realize how many other investors were losing their money in ways they didn't understand.

When I was 40, I decided to make a career of helping as many people as possible do better with their money. That desire became my life's work, and it remains my greatest passion today.

The idea for this book was born when I received an invitation from the Public Broadcasting Service, better known as PBS, to do a special presentation focused on how Americans can take better care of themselves financially. I was delighted to have this opportunity to speak to a very wide audience and support PBS at the same time.

Thousands of members of the baby boom generation are reaching age 65 every day, and most of them don't have enough money to continue the lifestyles they are used to.

The Employee Benefit Research Institute reported recently that American workers from age 55 to 64 have average retirement savings of $69,127. According to a rule of thumb widely used by financial planners, that's enough to add only about $230 a month to a retirement income on top of Social Security, pensions, and other sources.

As a nation, our financial fitness is relatively poor.

Investors Have Questions

I don't have to look any farther than my e-mail inbox to see the many ways that investing trips people up. Here are some of the many questions I received while I was writing this book.

Investors Have Trouble with Things That Are in Their Control

Janice wrote to say:

> We have been following your recommended strategy for several years. However, my husband got spooked during the Egypt/Mideast unrest and the rapid rise in oil prices, and he sold all our index funds. Since then the market has risen more than 700 points, and my husband now sees his error. Here are my questions: When do I get back into the market? Do I wait until there is a correction? Do I just jump in now? I need help.

Unfortunately, there is no good answer for Janice and her husband. After you jump off a moving train, it continues down the tracks, and that's what her husband did. They believe that he "now sees his error." But I wonder. What would she be saying if the market had just dropped 700 points instead of rising 700 points? Would they regard his sale of their index funds as an error—or as a savvy move that kept them from losing money? Either way, I suspect she would still be distressed, wondering when to put the money back in the market.

The quick answer is to follow a short but reliable rule for timing your investments: Buy when you have the money, and sell when you need the money.

Investors Have Trouble with Things That Are Completely Beyond Their Control

Here's an e-mail I got from Ben, an investor:

> I believe our government is heading down a path to ruin our currency and our country. Given the path that we are on, what are you doing to modify your fund recommendations?

If success required investors to change course with every new belief or prediction concerning the market, the economy, or the government, investors would never find any peace, and "long term" would be a concept for fools.

The research staff at my company is constantly evaluating potential opportunities and potential dangers. For more than 15 years our asset allocation recommendations have been largely unchanged. You can find those recommendations and the reasons for them in Appendix C, "The Ultimate Buy-and-Hold Strategy," which every serious investor should read. The changes we have made over the years consist of fine-tuning a general approach that we continue to believe will work.

Ben is feeling the effects of our 24/7 news cycle, including multiple cable channels that focus on finance. Even though on the surface we seem to have more information to help us make better decisions, in some ways just the opposite has happened. I'm a strong advocate of information and education. But this always-on information pipeline can overwhelm our brains. Trying to make sense of it can be like trying to take a drink from a fire hose. I believe this leads many people to pursue what I regard as an unproductive path.

The polarization of today's political and economic commentary encourages investors to become upset about trends and forces they cannot control. And this in turn has paralyzed many people emotionally, preventing them from making good decisions about the things they *can* control.

Even Investors with Money Don't Always Understand Financial Basics

Confusion can lead investors to take huge risks without realizing it. An investor named Rob sent me the following:

> I am 60 years old and very fortunate to have a total investment portfolio of $2.3 million, of which 60 percent is rental real estate, mostly apartment buildings and parking lots. The other 40 percent of my portfolio is invested in stock funds. I currently live off of the rental income, which is very consistent. I have no bond holdings, and I tend to look at the real estate as the fixed-income piece of my portfolio. Do you think that is valid?

In a word, no. I think Rob is blind to the very high level of risk he is taking. He owns some businesses (apartments and parking lots). Because those businesses bring him consistent income, he wants to think of them as bond funds. Bond funds are meant to reduce the risk of investing, not increase that risk. If we exclude the real estate, as I think we should, his portfolio is 100 percent in stocks. He is exposed to much more risk than he realizes.

Your Long-Term Financial Future

A woman I met recently told me that most of her friends get their advice from stockbrokers—or at least they did until the 2008 market meltdown. Now, she said, her friends, most of whom are retired or nearing retirement, have lost confidence in brokers and are making decisions on their own.

If they've lost confidence in Wall Street, where should they turn for trustworthy guidance? That may be the most important choice you will make as an investor. That issue is the centerpiece of this book.

We'll also be discussing several other forks in the road that play a big part in determining your long-term financial future, including:

- Will you try to beat the market or will you accept market returns?
- Will you carefully control how much risk you take?
- Will you diversify your investments widely and carefully?
- Will you insulate your investments from misguided emotional decisions?

Some people believe investing is so difficult that they won't be able to do it right. But in fact the opposite is true. Each of these important choices is relatively simple if you are willing to educate yourself and then act on what you have learned.

Finally, I've also included a step-by-step process you can use to figure out where you are, where you need to go, and what you need to do in order to get there. This series of exercises, located in Chapter 10, "Twelve Numbers to Change Your Life," will be particularly helpful to anyone who's within 10 to 15 years of retirement.

I'm a numbers guy. My recommendations are based on the numbers and the evidence. The quantitative side of life appeals to my brain. I live and breathe the question: "Where's the evidence?" My 2008 book *Live It Up Without Outliving Your Money!* leaned heavily on numbers and statistics in making the case for what I consider the best investment decisions.

However, I know that tables of numbers are a barrier for many people, a barrier that can keep them from learning the most important things they should know. After the crippling bear market of late 2007 through early 2009 and the subsequent recession, I wanted to find a way to give investors the best help I can without getting them bogged down. This book is the result.

In one sense I have combined two books into one. The "first book" consists of 11 chapters designed to make the information as accessible as possible to the widest audience. For readers who want the evidence and more details, the "second book" consists of Appendixes A–I.

It will take some time and attention for you to learn what's in this book and to achieve and maintain your financial fitness. But all worthwhile pursuits require you to invest time and attention.

- I once calculated that it takes the average person about 16,000 hours to get through primary and secondary school and obtain a bachelor's degree.

- Right now many doctors believe that if you want to be physically fit, you can do it by walking for one hour a day for a year. If you go back after one year, they may tell you to do the same thing for another year. That's 730 hours right there, and it never ends.

- I believe that once you have learned what's in this book, it should take you no more than 20 hours to set up your investments to take care of you for life. If you spend another two hours a year for maintenance, you'll stay financially fit. And you won't have to wash any sweaty clothes.

This book contains the knowledge I've gained in many thousands of hours spread over nearly half a century. It also contains my recipe for an action plan. When you have knowledge and action, you are well on your way to success.

However, there's another level that's available to investors. You might think of it as peace of mind, and you might think of it as wisdom.

I believe the final chapter in this book contains a lot of wisdom, and it didn't come from me. It came from a group of seasoned investment advisors who have spent many years working with real investors, many of them just like the ones who wrote the e-mail messages I quoted earlier.

That final chapter contains good news for all of us who struggle to do the best that we can. As it turns out, success in investing, like success in the rest of life, is under our control more than we probably think.

FINANCIAL FITNESS FOREVER

1

HOW DID
WE GET HERE?

"The future ain't what it used to be."
—*Yogi Berra*

It feels very strange to me to begin a book with a chapter of bad news. I'm a positive guy, an optimist who looks forward to the future. I believe we can have a future that's filled with interesting and fulfilling possibilities. But for reasons I'm going to outline in this chapter, that future belongs increasingly only to those of us who make the right choices and take care of ourselves.

We're in an emotional and financial fix, and in order to know how to get out of it, we should look at how we got into it. In a nutshell, we don't have enough money. Unlike our parents and grandparents, we probably don't have pensions. We have more debt than we can handle. Inflation invisibly and unrelentingly erodes our paychecks and our savings. We are trying to fix things the wrong ways.

It's easy to find financial advice to save more money and work longer. Those are both good pieces of advice, but not everybody can save more. And, most of us simply can't work for the rest of our lives.

What is less common is advice to be smarter investors. But for the rest of our lives, whatever our age and whatever our assets, the single most important thing we can do for the financial future of our families is to make better choices, which, in turn, will make us better investors. If we invest more intelligently, we can keep more of what we have saved and make the most of our savings.

A couple of generations ago, our society took better care of us in some ways. But now in the second decade of the 21st century, the security that our parents and grandparents took for granted has eroded. Millions of Americans are retired or on the brink of retirement without enough resources to continue the lifestyles they enjoyed for years.

Years ago, it was not unusual for multiple family generations to share households. This still is common in many less-developed countries. But in the United States, the practice waned as gradually rising wealth allowed younger people to move out and their parents to stay where they were. But now? The Pew Research Center and AARP reported in 2011 that multigenerational housing is returning. In 2000, about 4.8 percent of all households included multiple generations. A decade later, the number had increased to 6.1 percent, an addition of about 1.8 million such households.

I think it's safe to say that much of this increase was dictated by economic distress.

The Rand Corporation Center for the Study of Aging reported that, since the housing and financial markets began to collapse in 2007, approximately 39 percent of all Americans fell into one or more of the following traps. They had their homes foreclosed, had no job, owed more on their mortgages than their homes were worth, or were two or more months behind on their mortgages.

The center did a study focusing on how people were helping each other, mostly family and friends, get through the economic crisis that extended from 2007 through 2010. One thing it found was that the vast majority of the economic help went from parents to their grown children. More than 40 percent of the households headed by people age 50 to 69 reported giving financial help to younger households.

If you're a parent, that might not surprise you. But maybe it should.

Many of the trends that have been brewing in this country over the past 40 years were aptly summed up by a 69-year-old woman from Vermont. In a letter to her U.S. senator, she observed: "We are the first generation to leave our kids worse off than we were."

Practically forever, Americans have looked forward to enjoying more prosperity than their parents had. This became an article of faith, something so obvious that few people questioned it. What happened to reverse this very long trend?

The Way It Used to Be

I became an adult in the 1960s, and that has shaped my perspective. So I want to briefly paint the picture of financial life back then, when I joined Wall Street as a broker-in-training.

Most people expected to retire with pensions and Social Security to augment their modest savings. By today's standards, the tools and information available to investors of the 1960s were primitive. There were no 401(k) plans, no individual retirement accounts (IRAs), no discount brokers, very few no-load mutual funds, and no money-market funds. Exchange-traded funds (ETFs) and index funds, two low-cost products that are good for investors, didn't exist.

Sales commissions on stocks and bonds were regulated, at high rates that were conveniently favorable to Wall Street. Mutual funds were sold with sales loads of 8.5 percent, and brokers generally shunned the few fund families that dared to pay lower commissions. Fund commissions weren't applied only to purchases but were charged on reinvestments of dividends and capital gains distributions. In fact, when money-market funds were introduced, Wall Street tried to impose 8.5 percent sales commissions on them.

Ticker-tape machines were very common, many of them sounding like the tote boards at racetracks where odds were posted on horses. In a way, that was appropriate, as many people regarded investing as a game that required one to pick winning stocks.

Many brokers took home easy money not from being smart, helpful advisors but from the profits they could make on huge spreads between bid and ask prices. It wasn't uncommon for an illiquid stock to trade with a bid price of $9 and an ask price of $10, on each trade.

With no Internet or other electronic communications, information and knowledge moved slowly, making it easy for some investors to gain an advantage over others. Investing advice for the average American was available only in Sylvia Porter's newspaper column and monthly issues of Kiplinger's magazine, *Changing Times*. There was no *Money Magazine*. There was no Morningstar, no widely known academic research about investment returns. Almost nobody was teaching what is obvious today and was just as true then: If you pay more in expenses or taxes or sales commissions, you earn less on your investments. This is elementary-school math!

This lack of information made it easy for brokers to make money because most of their clients didn't have a clue. Now we investors know a lot more, so we should be much better off, right? Yes and no. Careful investors can easily tap into knowledge and tools to make their money work hard for them—and by that I don't necessarily mean an aggressive equity portfolio. Your money works hard for you only when it works *for you*, which means a portfolio that fits your needs and keeps your costs low.

On the other hand, Wall Street knows that many people aren't careful enough to protect themselves. As financial products have become ever more complex, the industry has developed new ways to take advantage of investors who are easily swayed by improbable promises of high returns and low risks.

In the 1960s, the prevailing investment advice was centered around picking individual stocks and, sometimes, buying individual bonds. Nobody had much understanding about the benefits, risks, and limits of diversification. Owning 15 to 20 stocks (most likely all of them U.S. companies) was considered ample diversification.

There was no talk of asset classes, and only a few investment firms followed strategies even slightly similar to what we think of today as value investing. Young brokers like me were trained to "sell to the path of least resistance," recommending what customers wanted to own. That meant stocks of well-known blue-chip companies. The most popular ones back then included old-time industrials like Sears and AT&T, up-and-coming technology stocks like Xerox and Digital Equipment—and an energy company called King Resources, which wound up in many portfolios mostly because so many brokers had been heavily wined and dined at the company's Sun Belt facilities.

If customers wanted to buy something out of the ordinary, turning them away would just give the commission to somebody else. For many people in the financial industry, this was a comfortable era in which to make money. Bankers almost never worked on weekends, and many of them could plan on easy lives that let them hit the golf course by 4 P.M. on many weekdays.

Everything Started to Change

The 1960s saw the start of a multifaceted upheaval in our society. Our president, his brother, and Martin Luther King Jr. were all assassinated within a half dozen years. Congress passed major civil rights legislation, and the Great Society was born, bringing new federal benefits to young (Head Start) and old (Medicare) alike. Major cities burned in riots. The war in Vietnam toppled another president, and the nightly television news brought images of dying soldiers and protests led by strangely dressed hippies into American living rooms—in color—for the first time.

Inflation, barely an issue at 2.4 percent for the 1960s, heated up, along with energy prices, in the 1970s. By the late 1970s and early 1980s, many Americans could only scratch their heads as they made payments on their 7 percent mortgages while the same banks offered 17 percent interest on 30-month CDs and wrote new home loans at 18 percent.

By the mid-1980s, inflation and interest rates started a long downward slide that kept going, to nearly everybody's astonishment, almost all the way to zero. Because bond prices rise when interest rates fall, many people acquired the mistaken belief that fixed-income funds were a form of growth investment.

In the 1960s, income tax rates dropped to 70 percent on taxable income more than $200,000. This seemed terribly high to me, though I didn't make anything close to that much money. But some of my firm's wealthy clients were quite pleased that they were no longer paying a top rate of 91 percent.

Later, tax rates kept coming down, and in the 1980s U.S. stock dividends and capital gains were taxed at preferred rates. This was supposed to reward the rich (officially for being rich and unofficially for being good political contributors) and at the same time encourage the rest of us to save and invest.

Simultaneously, the government introduced the 401(k) plan and the IRA, designed to let Americans defer taxes on their retirement savings while many of their employers unburdened themselves from the obligations of providing pensions. On the one hand, this was a great benefit, giving us incentives to automatically save money every payday. But on the other hand, it transferred the risks of investing away from employers and into the hands of employees.

Under the old model, a defined-benefit plan, the employer promises a monthly pension after so many years of service. The employer takes the risk that the pension fund's investments may produce a shortfall. This long-standing paternalistic model rewarded long service and let people know what they could count on. The best plans promised benefits adjusted to keep up with inflation.

But in the heavy inflation of the 1970s, that became quite a burden on pension funds.

Under the new model, the defined-contribution plan, the risks, rewards, and responsibilities of retirement investing belong to the employee. We didn't get raises to help us with this, but many employers offered to match part of whatever we contributed from our paychecks. These matching contributions may look like generous encouragement, but there's more going on than pure generosity. The laws governing 401(k) and similar retirement plans won't let highly paid executives take advantage of this tax deferral unless employees choose to do so as well.

While this was happening, a new world of investment opportunities opened up to investors.

- Despite fierce opposition from the Old Wall Street, discount brokerages began letting investors trade at deeply discounted commissions.
- The index fund was invented, letting investors bypass active management and participate directly in stock and bond indexes.
- Money-market funds were introduced with prices fixed at $1 a share, giving us alternatives to putting our money in individual bonds and bank savings accounts.
- The number of mutual funds exploded. In 1965, there were 170, with total assets of $35 billion in about 6.7 million accounts. Now there are more than 7,500, a number that's much higher if you count all the variations in share classes and ways you can purchase essentially the same fund. In 2009, mutual funds held roughly $11 trillion in 271 million accounts.
- Most mutual funds reduced their sales loads, and many had no loads at all, making it much more efficient for investors to own part of their portfolios. Old Wall Street didn't like this change.
- A wealth of new information available—first through newsletters, then by fax machines, and then online—took away Old Wall Street's monopoly on knowledge. With nearly instantaneous (and inexpensive) communications linking markets around the globe, today's investors can buy and sell securities any time they choose.

The Way It Has Become

The changes continue, of course. Now we have target-date retirement funds, many variations of variable annuities, ETFs, and 529 plans for college savings. With all these innovations, you might expect investors to be in relative heaven. We should be saving more money, doing a better job of investing it, and taking a more active and successful role in planning our retirements.

Lower taxes, lower commissions, and better investment options should have led us to save more. However, we are doing just the opposite. In 1981, U.S. households collectively saved about 12 percent of their income. By 2005, our savings rate was a negative 0.5 percent as we piled on more debt.

Instead of saving more, we were spending more. Easy credit, mass advertising, sophisticated marketing research, and fancy new products all competed very successfully to attract our money.

Commercial interests, fanned by a rapidly growing media, worked hard to teach us to equate money—especially the spending of it—with happiness. And they did a pretty good job.

Falling mortgage rates, looser regulations, and a thriving re-fi industry combined to induce us to start seeing our houses as piggybanks. Everybody "knew" housing prices would keep going up as our population expanded. Home equity came to be regarded as a "stagnant asset" that, if we could unlock it, would let us have new boats, destination weddings, remodeled kitchens, fancy cars, plastic surgery, home theaters, and personal computers—the list could go on and on. To the rescue came the home equity line of credit, complete with a checkbook.

However, the burden of all this spending caught up with many people, and the two-income household, once an anomaly, has become the norm. The results are starting to catch up with the baby boom generation.

For most financial planners trying to help people in their late 50s and early 60s, the pivotal question comes down to some variation of this: Are you ready to retire? In plain English, that means: Do you (or will you) have enough money to last the rest of your life if you stop working?

For many people, the best measure of retirement savings is the balance in the 401(k) or similar plan that is owned by approximately 60 percent of households nearing retirement age.

In 2011, the *Wall Street Journal* reported the median household headed by a 401(k) participant age 60 to 62 had less than one-quarter of the savings necessary to maintain its standard of living in retirement. This was based on estimates of 401(k) balances at the end of 2010 and salaries in 2009, all analyzed for the *Journal* by Boston College's Center for Retirement Research.

Even when Social Security, pensions, and estimated other savings were taken into account, at the end of 2010 most 401(k) participants didn't have enough to provide 85 percent of their 2009 incomes.

There are lots of reasons for this shortfall. Some people lose their jobs or have bona fide emergencies that rob them of their ability to save and force them to tap into savings prematurely. Others wait too long to start saving or underestimate the amount they'll need to save. Some borrow against their 401(k) plans, not realizing how difficult it will be to catch up later.

Some people invest their retirement savings unwisely, taking much too much risk or no risk at all. When 401(k) plans were relatively new in the late 1980s and early 1990s, it was not uncommon for employees to sign up using default investment choices that were the equivalent of money-market funds. By the time some boomers figured out what they had done, they had already thrown away half a decade or more of potential growth—time they could never get back.

The Center for Retirement Research, according to the *Journal*, found that the median household headed by people age 60 to 62 had 401(k) plan balances of $149,400. In order to retire with 85 percent of their preretirement income, they needed that money to generate income of $39,465 a year. That is a withdrawal rate of 26.4 percent, more than five times the rate that most financial planners consider prudent for people retiring at age 65.

For many American households, retirement won't be anything like what they had wanted or planned. For some, it is a financial disaster just waiting to happen.

While all this has been going on, our government hasn't exactly set an inspiring example. It seemed to me when I was growing up that our political leaders tried to lead us into a better future for the common good. I get less of that feeling now. Leaders on both sides of the political aisle seem to be more interested in finding ways to spend money and getting somebody else to pay for it. Who that "somebody else" is, however, is never made clear.

At the start of the 21st century, the United States had regular, growing budget surpluses large enough to lead some economists to predict we would be able in our lifetimes to retire the national debt—the equivalent of a household paying off its 30-year mortgage.

But did our government pursue such a path? Hardly. Instead, taxes were reduced and spending was increased. Our national debt has ballooned to unprecedented levels. Who will wind up paying this piper? I'm afraid it will be our kids and grandkids.

More than 60 percent of today's college and university students borrow money to pay for their education. Student loan debt now totals about $850 billion, more than the nation's total credit card debt. While their parents finance and refinance their homes with mortgages at less than 4 percent interest, some recent graduates are paying more than 8 percent on their student loans.

When I entered the investment business in the 1960s, most people told me their primary financial goals included leaving something for their kids when they were gone. These days, I don't hear that mentioned nearly as often. More likely, people will tell me their hope is to live well themselves and not to be a burden to their kids. This may seem subtle, but it's a big change.

What does all this mean to us as investors? I believe that globalization is putting pressure on U.S. corporations and our government to cut benefits and compensation for workers. Increasingly, U.S. corporations believe their primary responsibility is to build the best product at the lowest possible cost so they can maximize profits to shareholders.

Sometimes that means the product will be built here. But ever since I was in college, transportation and communications have been shrinking the world. Too often, the best product can be built for the best price somewhere outside the United States. No longer can we count on our employers and our government to take care of us.

More and more, we are the ones responsible for our own financial security. That sounds like bad news. But it comes bundled along with news that's good, at least for Americans who know what to do with the new ways we can invest our retirement savings.

We have the 403(b), the 401(k), the Roth 401(k), the Simple IRA, the traditional IRA, the Roth IRA, and Roth conversions available to everyone. The limits have been raised to allow higher contributions into all these retirement plans.

More good news! New and improved investment products make investing easier, more accessible, and (sometimes) less expensive. These improvements include target-date retirement funds, ETFs, and more choices in index funds.

Still more good news! Employees are starting to demand better investment options within their retirement plans. Many new employees are now signed up automatically for 401(k) and similar plans unless they specifically choose to opt out. That means more people are saving for retirement and thinking ahead.

But the news isn't totally positive. Human behavior hasn't changed. Investors make the same emotional mistakes they did 50 years ago. To get the most benefit from all the tools available to us, we have to find ways to overcome emotional hurdles and financial hurdles. We need to learn what's most important and then find ways to put that knowledge into practice. We need to take our futures back by making better decisions.

We can do it, and this book is a road map into a financially fit future that will be good for us, good for our children, and good for our country.

2

ARE WE OUR OWN WORST ENEMIES?

"If you want to see the greatest threat to your financial
future, go home and take a look in the mirror."
—*Jonathan Clements*

In addition to the systemic problems described in Chapter 1, "How Did We Get Here?," would-be successful investors must confront human nature. And human nature, to put it mildly, isn't always our friend.

If you've ever watched people try to diet or make new habits (or if you've tried this yourself), you know there's a Grand Canyon of difference between what people know they should do and what they actually do. In this chapter, we'll explore some of the reasons why that's true.

Wall Street and Madison Avenue know human nature very well, and they use tricks and sophisticated sales techniques to exploit our weak spots. We won't always win this tug-of-war, but we will improve our chances of success if we know ourselves better.

We live in a social and economic system that encourages us to be crazy when it comes to money. As kids we were taught by television and radio ads that we should beg our parents to buy us things we didn't need. As adults we're constantly told we should spend money we don't have and incur debt we cannot afford to repay. We are encouraged to think we can buy happiness and peace of mind, when in fact those commodities are not for sale.

Banks spend millions of advertising dollars to get our kids hooked on credit while they're in college. Advertising and media encourage us to never be satisfied, to crave the latest, to follow expensive fads in virtually every part of life. We complain about high gasoline prices while we pay more per gallon for drinking water, much of it taken right from the public taps. We spend millions on sports stadiums while our public schools deteriorate for lack of money. The media lures us to be outraged over things that are outside our control.

Our brains are wired to lead us astray in many ways. In every part of our lives we make dumb decisions about what will be good for us, often choosing what we think will bring us short-term pleasure even when we know it may very well bring us long-term pain. We are overconfident and find it extremely difficult to read, listen, and think critically. In these and other ways, we make our lives more difficult than they need to be.

This chapter is an introduction to the science of behavioral economics. You probably will recognize things about yourself, and that's to be expected. You will be a better investor if you understand some of this psychology.

Rationality

When economics was a new concept, the science was built on the assumption that humans behave like machines. In this unrealistic model, our economic behavior is totally rational and not influenced by emotions. We know everything that's relevant and have unlimited willpower; therefore, we will always do "the right thing." If all this were really true, nobody would ever spend, eat, or drink too much. We would always save enough, work enough, and exercise enough. Right!

Stuck with these assumptions, economists had a terrible time explaining real-life behavior. Thus was born behavioral economics and behavioral finance, which take psychology into account in understanding what we do and why we do it. As MarketWatch.com (http://www .marketwatch.com) columnist Mark Hulbert has said, "When it comes to investment decisions, your emotions always trump your intellect." This goes far beyond the old Wall Street saying (which contains a lot of truth) that the market is driven by greed and fear.

Here are some of the key findings of behavioral finance research:

- We often follow rules of thumb instead of logic.
- We assume that whatever is happening right now is likely to continue happening far into the future.
- We explain events using our personal experiences and stereotypes instead of reason.

- We give more importance to new information ("the news") than to things we've known for a long time. The recent past seems much more important than the past 50 years.
- We would rather have an answer, even if it's the wrong answer, than be left with a question.
- We look for—and usually find—what we think are meaningful patterns in random events.
- We think we are luckier, more skillful, and more insightful than in fact we are.
- We have a herd mentality, and we are overly influenced by what other people are doing, even in the face of compelling evidence that this is contrary to our best interests.
- We fail to understand statistics and probabilities.

As a result of all these points, we often think we're being quite rational as we make counterproductive decisions.

Levels of Risk

One of the most important things many investors should do is reduce their levels of risk. (We will talk about that again later.) But sometimes when we do this, our nuttiness takes over.

A famous case in point involves an experiment with 200 taxicabs in New York City, a place where even minor collisions tie up traffic, fry passengers' tempers, and cost cabbies money. A group of taxicabs was outfitted with brakes that were noticeably better than those on most other cabs. These cabs were carefully monitored for several months, and the officials in charge of the experiment believed the cabs would be involved in fewer accidents. Instead, officials were startled to find that the cabs with the better brakes actually had slightly *more* collisions than those with the same old brakes.

What was going on? It turned out that cabbies knew they had gained more ability to stop and decided to "spend" that gain by simply driving faster. Some investors do essentially the same thing when they increase their holdings of bond funds and cash and then "bet the farm" on risky investments.

Malcolm Gladwell, author of *What the Dog Saw and Other Adventures,* described it this way: "If roads are wider, then people will drive faster. If a car has antilock brakes, a driver is more likely to tailgate and brake more abruptly. If cars can better protect drivers in the event of an accident, people will drive faster." Despite the best risk management strategies and tools, our behavior is likely to change to keep our overall level of risk unchanged at a level with which we are comfortable.

One book, to say nothing of a single chapter, is insufficient to cover all the ways we are nuts. But I'd like to cover some high points that I think apply to investors. You'll find a more detailed discussion in a book I recommend often, *Your Money and Your Brain* by Jason Zweig.

Although I don't recommend investing in individual stocks, they are relatively simple and provide a good laboratory to look at how we think and behave as investors. That's why I'll use stocks to illustrate some of the following points. But I hope you'll remember that in my view, the very act of owning an individual stock is irrational.

Our brains sometimes get confused, not knowing the difference between what we think and what we feel. When we buy a stock, we usually do so with great anticipation, hoping we've made a brilliant decision.

Some eager investors watch the price every hour on the first day they own it and then daily after that for a while. And it's well documented that some investors tend to place a great deal of importance on how an investment behaves soon after they buy it. Maybe it's a form of bonding.

Acme Bubblegum

If you buy Acme Bubblegum (a corporate name I made up) stock for $20 a share and within two weeks it is selling for $23, you are likely to believe you were very smart and you've got "a winner." If it stays at or above that $23 level for a month or more, you may decide you can "trust" the stock.

This works in the opposite direction, too. If Acme stock sinks to $17 a few weeks after you buy it, you're likely to think you've made a big mistake. And if it stays below your purchase price for long, you may "lose trust" in that stock.

Emotionally this may seem sensible, but it's really nonsense. "Trust" a stock? That stock doesn't know you own it, doesn't care about you, doesn't have any obligation to you. In fact, it doesn't even know you exist. That stock you may come to love or hate is just a tiny piece of some business. Its price can change thousands of times every trading day, depending on supply and demand. When you start ascribing human qualities to such a thing, you will almost certainly make bad decisions.

Gut Feelings

Investors often rely on their gut feelings when they make buy and sell decisions. Gut feelings, sometimes collectively known as intuition, are extremely useful for making judgments about lots of situations, especially those that involve threats of danger. Our brains are hardwired to instantly size up a situation and its potential to affect us. Even before we know what we're looking at, we can swerve to avoid an object in the road when we're driving.

This is an amazing talent on the highway. But it does us no good when we try to apply it to something complex and conceptual like Acme Bubblegum stock.

Successful investing demands analysis and careful thinking much more than gut reactions. As Zweig says in *Your Money and Your Brain,* "One of the clearest signals that you are wrong about an investment is having a hunch that you're right about it."

Changes

Our brains are highly developed to respond to changes while ignoring what remains constant. The most widely quoted investment indicator is the Dow Jones Industrial Average, which at this writing is a bit more than 12,000. When this average goes up or down by 100 or 200 points in a day, investors (and news broadcasters and commentators) place great emphasis on the tiny part that changed, not the overwhelming part that didn't.

A 200-point fall in the index represents only about 1.7 percent of the value—equivalent to less than two cents on the dollar. Yet if you listened to the evening news without knowing the numbers, you might think that the market stumbled by 10 or 15 percent. Your emotions might go into high gear, urging your brain to do something to protect yourself from a "threat." But in reality, the event is more likely to be part of the normal noise of market trading.

If you apply this to your whole portfolio, you may be led astray even faster. If your nest egg is worth $300,000 and it rises by $3,000 in a day, you'll likely feel richer and smarter. Just think, a "free" $3,000 fell into your lap today. The change seems very important, but in fact it's just the equivalent of having a $1 bill suddenly be worth $1.01. And never mind that your newly minted $3,000 is just as likely to vanish tomorrow as the market moves up and down.

Changing the Subject

Return for a moment to Acme Bubblegum. If you're trying to figure out whether to buy it (or, if you already own it, whether to sell it), a truly informed and rational decision requires lots of information and understanding that could take you months or even years to acquire. Yet you're looking at the stock today, and you like it. In order to make the buy-or-sell decision, your brain has to have something simpler.

Without realizing what you're doing, you are likely to reframe the question. In effect, you will be changing the subject without realizing it. You *should* be asking yourself about the industry, the competition, the management and its strategy, and the anticipated demand for bubblegum. But those are hard questions. So instead you may very well ask yourself much simpler ones like these:

- Do I like this company's product?
- Do my kids like this product?
- Have I seen this product on the shelves of lots of convenience stores?
- Do I have a good (or bad) feeling about the recent movements of the stock price?
- Did I just hear or read something positive (or negative) about this stock?

The chances are high that by the time you have this much interest in that stock, you want to either buy it or sell it. Your brain, wishing you to have what you want, jumps through whatever hoops are necessary in order to justify your desired behavior. The result is you do what you want, and you have "good reasons" to support your decision.

That's a pretty good example of the perpetual tug-of-war between thinking and feeling.

Paying Attention

Sometimes, we're in such a rush to get in on the action that we don't even pay attention to what we're doing. This includes sophisticated professional investors as well as individuals. Zweig cites two famous examples. The first illustrates pure sloppiness. The second illustrates the combination of greed, speed, and . . . let's call the third ingredient ignorance.

- On October 1, 1997, the price of Massmutual Corporate Investors stock rose 2.4 percent on extremely heavy trading volume. Nothing at all had changed about that company, so why did this happen? As it turns out, that was the very day that another company, WorldCom, announced a takeover bid to acquire MCI Communications. MCI and Massmutual were totally unrelated except for one thing: Massmutual's stock ticker symbol was "MCI." Hundreds of investors were so eager to cash in on WorldCom's takeover bid that they didn't stop for even 10 seconds to think before issuing instructions to "buy MCI." (Many of them probably typed that ticker symbol into their computers directly. The computers, of course, had no way to question what they were doing.) What those eager investors should have said was "buy MCIC" because that was the ticker symbol of the company they thought they were buying.

- In 1999, near the peak of the technology boom, a company named Mannatech Inc. offered its stock to the public for the first time. The price shot up 368 percent in its first two days of trading after this initial public offering as greedy investors mistakenly assumed from the company's name that it was in some red-hot part of the Internet business. Had those investors done even the most basic homework, they could have easily learned that Mannatech was a marketer of laxatives and nutritional supplements. (For an interesting mental exercise, imagine that you were one of the original owners of Mannatech stock who bought it expecting nothing more than a reasonable long-term return. What should you do when the stock goes through the roof in two days for no apparent reason? Should you sell when you can double your money and then kick yourself for getting out too soon? Should you sell when you can triple your money? Or should you just hang on and do nothing, only to watch over the next few days as the stock loses almost all the "new value" it had suddenly acquired? There's no right answer to this one!)

I wish I could tell you these stories are unusual one-time blips. But human beings don't pay nearly as much attention to what's going on around them as they think they do.

In his 2006 book, *Stumbling on Happiness,* Harvard psychologist Daniel Gilbert describes a study in which a subject was instructed to approach a stranger on a college campus and ask for directions to a particular building. While the subject and the stranger were studying a campus map, two construction workers, each holding one end of a large door, rudely cut between the researcher and the stranger.

This was planned as part of the experiment so that for a moment, the stranger could not see the person who had asked for directions. In just a few seconds, as the "construction workers" passed by, the person who had been asking for directions ducked behind the door and walked off out of sight from the stranger while a *new* "stranger" who had been hiding behind the door took the place of the original person and picked up the conversation. The new person was of a different height, wore different clothes, and had a different voice and haircut from the original.

If you were the subject who had been asked for help, you would be very startled by this, right? Well, maybe not. As this experiment was repeated, time after time most of the Good Samaritan subjects didn't even notice they were suddenly talking to somebody entirely different.

When an important and obvious part of the world that's right before our eyes suddenly changes and we don't even notice, how are we to trust our senses?

Emotional Candy

Making a profit has a curious effect on our brains. It sometimes gives us such an emotional high that it can blot out reality. If you own five stocks and four of them do nothing or incur losses, but the fifth one doubles in value, you will focus almost exclusively on that fifth stock and begin to regard yourself as someone who makes shrewd investments and doubles your money.

Even if your total stock value is virtually unchanged, you will remember the double. So far, that's fine—a bit of emotional candy for your mind. But if you aren't careful, the desire for that "big killing" will start dictating your behavior as you gloat over your insight and instincts. Worse, you won't know your actual performance, a fact that's vital if you want to live in the real world instead of your fantasy world.

Our brains are so addicted to emotional highs that we care more about how much money we might conceivably make (buying Lotto tickets, for example, when the jackpot is huge) than we care about the probability of making anything at all.

In reality, the more Lotto tickets you buy, the more likely you are to lose. Wonder why? If you bought every single ticket in a certain game, you'd be guaranteed to win the jackpot. But because the game ultimately benefits the house, you would have paid more for that jackpot than what it was worth. You could brag to your friends about winning the jackpot, but if you told them what it cost you, you'd have to admit that you were a loser.

Experts

Even though thousands of studies have shown that experts don't have any insight into the future, we are so eager to have answers that we can easily abandon our common sense.

Stock analysts are supposedly experts in the finances of the companies they follow, with personal relationships with top managers and sometimes undercover inside sources. These experts should at the very least be able to predict companies' earnings with some accuracy, right? David Dreman, an investor and author who founded a company that bears his name, tracked analysts' estimates of upcoming quarterly earnings over 30 years. He found that, on average, they were wrong by 41 percent.

The analysts always have reasons for not getting it right, and they don't get sacked for being wrong. Worse, investors keep on believing those analysts' predictions.

In some ways, successful investing requires you to be a contrarian. When everybody seems to "know" that disaster is looming, stock prices will be relatively low. If you're a long-term investor with faith in the future, this may hand you a great buying opportunity. But in order to buy what everybody else wants to dump, you have to buck the trend of conventional wisdom. That may make rational sense, but it feels very scary. When financial risk is the lowest, emotional risk is the highest.

Likewise, when everybody is certain that nothing can go wrong (remember the dot-com craze of the late 1990s), stock prices will be relatively high, presenting you with a good opportunity to lock in some profits by selling. If you sell at such a time, you may be making what will turn out to be a great financial decision. But how will you feel if the market goes up 5 percent the day after you sell? During what is meant to be a long-term process, the emotional tug of short-term results can be so strong that, if we allow it, our emotions will lead us into dumb decisions designed to bring us short-term relief, even at the cost of long-term pain.

Rat Brains Versus Human Brains

Many investors have an overwhelming belief that they can figure out how to predict short-term price movements, which in truth are largely random. Here's a behavioral finance experiment showing how futile this can be. A researcher sets up a screen onto which a light flashes repeatedly, each time showing up as either red or green. Four out of five times, the light is green, but the sequence is random. After each flash, the subjects are asked to guess which color will come up next. When rats do this experiment (with food as the reward for correct guesses), they fairly quickly figure out that they get the most rewards for always picking green. This, in fact, is the correct guessing strategy.

But most human subjects think they are smarter. Even after they have been told that the flashing is random and the light will be green four out of every five times, they try to do better. They pick green four out of five times instead of every time, reducing their accuracy on average to 68 percent. Often, after the subjects believe they have discovered patterns, they find that the longer they work at it, the worse their scores become.

I know this is insulting, but try this idea on for size. There's an important difference between rat brains and human brains. Humans want to figure things out, to detect patterns, to do the clever thing, above all, to be right. Rats just want results. (What's wrong with them, anyway?)

Overconfidence

If you ask a group of 100 people the following question, usually about 70 to 80 will raise their hands: "Compared with the other 99 people here, are you above average at (fill in the blank, whether it's looks, personality, cooking, golf, fishing, driving, telling jokes or intelligence)?"

Obviously, except for the mythical Lake Wobegon, three-quarters of us can't be above average. But we seem to believe that we are, and when that happens we behave as if that belief were true.

When he's speaking to groups of investors, Zweig sometimes hands out slips of paper and asks the audience to jot down two numbers: how much money they think they will have saved by the time they retire and how much money they think the average person in the room will have at retirement. Almost always he finds that people think they will save at least 1.8 times as much as the average person in the room.

Human nature includes a very strong tendency to think that we're better than we really are. Our brains are designed in some ways to reinforce this belief.

We can easily fool ourselves into thinking we have predicted whatever is happening. "I knew it," is a common phrase you'll hear if you listen for it. Sometimes we hear something like: "Anybody could have seen that coming." This is emotionally satisfying, but it's a logical trap.

In 1998 and 1999, most stock investors believed they "knew" that technology and telecommunications companies were reinventing the future. Those companies would be great investments and would help define the 21st century—if only we could get through the dreaded Y2K problem that might shut down the world's computers on January 1, 2000.

By the middle of 2001, millions of investors had invested in those stocks and had lost a ton of money in them. Many of these investors reported in 2001 that they had recognized technology as a bubble and had foreseen the crash. Ah, how easily we fool ourselves! And by the way, those investors also said they had never put much stock in the Y2K fears, which turned out to be mostly unjustified.

The trap I'm describing is the belief that we possess powers and capabilities that we don't have. Behavioral economists call this "hindsight bias." This fallacy makes it hard for us to learn from our mistakes. We just conveniently forget those mistakes or reinterpret them. More dangerous, this trap leads us to believe that we can see what's ahead. In a financial world that's heavily influenced by random events, that can be a recipe for disaster.

Zweig notes some of the many ways that we have an overwhelming bias toward optimism and ends his discussion with this observation: "Finally, in what may be the ultimate form of unrealistic optimism, 64 percent of Americans believe they will go to heaven after they die; only one half of 1 percent expect to go to hell." Fortunately or unfortunately, there is no way to measure the accuracy of these expectations.

Overconfidence can lead investors to do a lot of buying and selling. The portfolios of people who trade the most, on average, underperform those of people who trade the least—by about seven percentage points a year. Over time, that can make an overwhelming difference. If you invest $20,000 a year for 30 years and earn a return of 10 percent, your nest egg would be worth about $3.3 million. But if you invest the same $20,000 a year for 30 years and earn only 3 percent, you'll have only about $950,000.

In *Your Money and Your Brain*, Zweig tells a story on himself. In 1993 he was the mutual funds editor at *Forbes* and contributing 5 percent of his pay to his company retirement plan, although he could have put in twice that much. When a friend asked him why he didn't put in all that he could, Zweig answered, "Because I can do better with my money than they can, that's why." Unfortunately for him, he found that was wrong. Fifteen years later, he confesses, he calculated that his overconfidence had cost him at least $250,000.

Tolerating Risks

While Zweig embraced risks, some people tend to shun them. One morning in 1973, just a few minutes after Harvard economist Wassily Leontief learned he had won the Nobel Prize in economics, an Associated Press reporter asked him by phone what plans he might have for the $100,000 that would come with the prize. "Oh, I will just put that in the bank," he said without hesitation. "I love to speculate with ideas but never with money."

In other words, one of the world's most renowned economists knew instantly that he had zero tolerance for risk.

It's possible to calculate a rational and reasonable risk tolerance for just about anybody if you assume that person has no emotions or will pay absolutely no attention to an investment portfolio until it's time to use it. But in the real world, our risk tolerance is emotional, and it changes. In the midst of a bull market, it's easy to be brave. Yet time after time I've seen such bravado quickly turn to panic when the bull market turns into a bear market.

Many thousands of years ago, our human ancestors faced risks that were not conceptual at all: being attacked by a predator, running out of food or water, freezing in winter with inadequate clothing. If you failed to adequately respond to those risks, you might very well lose your life. Of course some of the perceived risks turned out to be false alarms.

When we misjudged a situation by underreacting, the penalty could be sudden death. Our brains gradually learned to avoid underreacting. But when we made the opposite mistake, overreacting to danger that wasn't real, there wasn't much of a penalty. In fact, when we discover there's no real threat behind our worries, we can experience the emotional reward of relief and peace. Even though overreacting was a mistake, our brains gradually learned that it wasn't a serious mistake. Consequently, we have evolved to become very sensitive to potential harm, with a built-in "better safe than sorry" approach to life.

This may be helpful when we deal with tigers and sharks. But it doesn't do us any favors as investors.

How we evaluate the seriousness of a risk depends in part on how it's presented or explained to us. Because our brains are hooked by emotional triggers, this can lead us to abandon logic. Researchers asked several hundred physicians to imagine that they were patients who had been diagnosed with cancer and had to choose whether or not to undergo surgery.

One group of doctors was told that experience with their condition indicated 10 out of every 100 patients could be expected to die in surgery. Another group was told that 90 out of every 100 patients would survive surgery. The facts were exactly the same. But one scenario was presented (or framed, as the researchers like to say) in terms of potential gain (survival) and the other was presented in terms of potential loss (death).

If you think doctors are totally rational, you might be surprised to learn that half the doctors in the first group (who had been told that 10 percent of patients would die in surgery) chose radiation instead, while in the second group (who had been told that 90 percent of patients would survive the surgery), only 16 percent chose radiation.

This may help explain why so many investors have trouble doing what will produce the better outcome for them. Wall Street says we should sometimes cut our losses, yet our emotional makeup tells us that if we sell a losing stock, we'll be making the loss "real." So sometimes we hang on when we shouldn't.

Unfortunately, our emotions also discourage us from rebalancing our portfolios to keep our risk in check. Rationally, this is the right thing to do, forcing us mechanically to buy low and sell high. But emotionally, this requires us to "punish" the very investments we have "learned to trust" and that have "treated us well" while we "reward" those that have been "beating us up."

If you need evidence that our intellect is not always in control, that's it. No wonder investing is tricky! When we have to struggle with relatively simple things like this, how will we survive when Wall Street spends an estimated $6 billion a year on advertising designed to manipulate our emotions?

What We Don't Know

Above all, we have a terrible time admitting when we don't know something. Nature abhors a vacuum, and the human mind despises the words "I don't know." Many people regard me as a pretty savvy investor and think I know what's coming. Yet whenever they ask me about the future, the only truly honest answer I can give them is, "I don't know."

I happen to think this is a very useful answer. If somebody with my experience and my appetite for knowledge can't know something so important, it's unlikely that anybody else can know it. But many people hate that answer and feel let down by it. Even highly experienced financial experts who understand this perfectly, when they're asked what the future holds, often feel obliged to make something up that sounds reasonable or defends their current holdings or recommendations.

If you'd like to learn more about the psychology of investing and instant gratification, you can look up a paper, "Unskilled and Unaware of It," I particularly like written by two professors at Cornell University. To find this paper online, go to a search engine and enter the names of the authors, David Dunning and Justin Kruger. They describe how the most competent people tend to underestimate their abilities and the least competent people tend to overestimate their abilities.

I want to end this chapter with a bit of advice. If you really want to improve your investing results, forget about the financial press and the financial TV. Instead, look in the mirror and ask yourself if you are you truly the above-average, unemotional superinvestor you think you are.

If you are that superinvestor, do you have convincing evidence? If not, are you willing to do what it takes to achieve above-average results? In the coming chapters, I'll show you exactly how to do that.

3

WHERE WILL YOU PLACE YOUR TRUST?

"An investment in knowledge pays the most interest."
—Benjamin Franklin

In 1963, U.S. television audiences became addicted to a new television game show called "Let's Make a Deal." The show became so popular that it was later syndicated, and it's still being shown in many countries around the globe.

On the show, contestants chosen from the audience were offered the chance to accept an unidentified prize that they knew would be moderately desirable, for example, a TV set or a refrigerator. They didn't know exactly what prize they would get because it was hidden behind a door. To make the game more interesting, the contestants could instead choose an unknown prize concealed behind one of two other doors. One of their choices was something much more desirable such as a new car or a vacation, but the other was something called a "zonk," a losing proposition that might be a roomful of junked furniture or an article of clothing in some ridiculous color or size.

The contestants had to choose between the unknown prize that they probably would like or take a chance of either getting a much better prize or getting something they probably wouldn't like at all.

Because this was television, the contestants were encouraged to behave as if this were among the most important choices they would ever make. It wasn't, but the show seemed to be fun for everybody. Bad guesses didn't have any lasting consequences except perhaps some public embarrassment.

In real life, many of the risks that we take are much more real. Fun isn't guaranteed. This book is about some fundamental choices that are much more important than those on any game show.

Let's Make a Deal

In this chapter, I'm going to ask you to choose one of three doors. The choice has consequences that can last a lifetime. That's the bad news. The good news is that you have one major advantage over the contestants on "Let's Make a Deal"—I'm going to show you what's behind each door.

If you get this choice right, most of the rest of investing will fall into place naturally, and you will be on your way to financial fitness forever. But if you get this choice wrong, no matter what else you do, you will be swimming upstream.

Most likely, you have never thought about this choice. I've read hundreds of books on investing, and I've never seen one that clearly identifies these three doors.

Success in investing, as I mentioned in the Introduction, is not terribly different from success in the rest of life. One of the most important things we do over and over again in our lives is place our trust in people to know what we don't know and to look out for our interests.

Very few of us have the resources, the time, the knowledge, or the patience to discover for ourselves everything we need to know in order to make our money do the most for us. We have to trust that somebody else has figured things out and has found answers that will work for us. The problem is that lots of people claim to know what is best for us, and they supply different answers. Who deserves to have our trust?

Most people and institutions want our trust, but not all of them are equally worthy of it. The brightest people I know are careful about whom they trust. I think it's fair to say that successful people generally make more good choices about this than unsuccessful people do.

In all my years in the investment business, I have found only three basic choices. Because they are so important, I've listed them here and will keep referring to them throughout the book.

- You can trust Wall Street, which in my mind includes most of the financial media as well as investment banks, insurance companies, brokerage houses, and mutual fund families.
- You can trust what I call Main Street, meaning your neighbors, friends, relatives, colleagues, and people you may meet casually.
- You can trust the academic community, which I have labeled University Street.

Imagine that each one of these groups of people is behind a door. Which door do you open for the best source of investment advice? Let's open those doors, which I have labeled Wall Street, Main Street, and University Street, and have a look. I think you'll see some things you didn't know were there.

For starters, it's pretty obvious that there are lots of people who want you to open Door #1, Wall Street, and lots of other people who hope you'll open Door #2, Main Street. Why do you suppose they want you to do that?

Door #1

Behind Door #1, Wall Street has an obvious agenda. Mutual fund companies, brokerage houses, independent advisors, banks, and insurance companies all want our business. In return for our trust (plus some of our assets), they offer assurances and carefully selected past performance data to "prove" they can make our future bright.

However, Wall Street is riddled with conflicts of interest along with hidden and undecipherable fees. Their smiling, friendly people will do virtually anything to attract our assets to their management. This is a path that leads to profits—profits for Wall Street. Wall Street wants us to trust their experts, wants us to try to beat the market—while Wall Street itself seeks opportunities to nibble away at our assets every step of the way.

Door #2

Behind Door #2, Main Street also has an agenda—but it's less obvious. Our friends, neighbors, colleagues, and relatives probably don't want a slice of our assets—at least not enough to come right out and ask for our money. Instead, they want us to respect them and understand how smart and savvy they are.

These people are happy to share their successes, their hot tips, their newest insights. Trouble is, they are amateurs who rarely if ever show us proof of their claims. Did your neighbor who bragged about his or her stock market prowess ever show you annual trading statements or personal tax returns? Probably not, and this means you really have no way to judge the validity of what you're being told.

Door #3

Behind Door #3, University Street has the most interesting agenda, one that doesn't actually involve us. Professors and graduate students want their peers to realize how brilliant they are to have figured out the intricacies of investing. They want their research to be published, with all the attendant opportunities that can result, including tenure, acclaim, and even the Nobel Prize.

The academics on University Street don't have much reason to care whether or not we know about them or follow their teachings. They aren't trying to impress us or make a profit from us. They're most interested in finding out what works and what doesn't—and where the holes are in Wall Street's sales pitches.

So it boils down to three choices: We can trust institutions that want us to help them make profits. We can trust people who want to impress us. Or we can trust people who don't care what we think about them—who just want to get it right. In my mind, the choice is clear. I'll take Door #3, and I think you should do the same.

In the rest of this chapter, I'll explain why.

Wall Street

I'm going to paint a picture of Wall Street that may seem very negative. It's certainly quite different from the impression you're likely to get from the upbeat ads and commercials for brokers, mutual funds, and insurance companies.

I want to emphasize a point here. My criticism is not directed at the individuals who work on Wall Street. My beef is with the system. Obviously, the financial world as we know it could not operate without brokers, buyers, sellers, traders, and all sorts of systems for gathering and disseminating information.

As investors, we need some version of Wall Street. But we need a better Wall Street. We need a Wall Street that's aligned with the interests of the investors whose money is at stake, whose futures are at stake. Until we get that better Wall Street, we have to be on our guard.

Most of us deal with brokers in one form or another. In the simplest terms, a broker is somebody who takes our buy orders and our sell orders and sees that they are executed. But brokers do much more than that. They sell products, often in the guise of giving advice.

When we walk into an automobile showroom, we understand that the salesperson who greets us is not there to be a transportation consultant. We know that salesperson's job is to persuade us to buy a car—and ideally to sign the papers before the day is done. In car sales, this is easy to figure out. Yet many investors never seem to figure out that the same thing is true of brokers. They are there to sell.

If you have a broker, you probably like him and trust him. (I use the male pronoun for writing convenience only; I know that many brokers are women.) And the chances are good that he deserves your trust. This may surprise you, so let me repeat it. Most brokers deserve your trust, at least as individuals.

The problem is that brokers don't work for themselves. They work for companies designed to generate profits. And we investors are the source of those profits. The danger to you is much more likely to be the broker's boss, the branch manager. And the boss's boss, perhaps a district manager too, and so on up the line including the CEO, board of directors, and shareholders. Up and down this long chain, do you know who really cares about you as a person? The answer is probably nobody except your broker. And your broker is the person with the least status and power in this system.

If your broker loses your trust and business, he probably won't lose his job. However, if your broker loses the trust of the people he reports to, he could find himself on the street. You can be sure your broker understands this. In a pinch, the company and its interests must prevail.

The company's interests are served when revenue is generated, most often from sales commissions.

Commissions often seem minor, a convenient way for you to pay for expert advice. But commissions can cause well-meaning sales professionals to recommend one product instead of another just because of the size of the commission.

Naturally, salespeople would rather earn larger commissions instead of smaller ones. And that's where the conflict of interest begins. Wall Street pays the highest commissions on the products that are hardest to sell. And those are the very things that people are most reluctant to buy because such products carry the highest risks.

Here's the point I want you to take away from this: Your broker has more financial incentives to persuade you to buy expensive and risky financial products than he does to get you to buy cheaper, safer ones.

Here are two stories to illustrate.

Some years ago I was invited to speak at a conference of agents who had been outstanding producers for a particular insurance company. At a cocktail party after a fabulous day in a location that could only be described as paradise, I got to chatting with one of the agents and asked how he and the others had qualified for the lavish honors and treatment they had received.

He was an independent agent and told me he had sold large amounts of one of the insurance company's products. He liked this product and found it was easy to sell and beneficial to his clients.

That was the good news. The bad news was that in order to win the trip to this conference, he had to sell an equal amount of one of the insurance company's other products. He did not believe this other product was in his clients' best interests. He sold that other product anyway in order to put money in his own pocket and take care of his family—and to win the trip to paradise.

I see a naked conflict of interest here. You want someone who will direct you to the products that will meet your needs in the best and most efficient way. But Wall Street wants to sell you high-commission products. When Wall Street gets its way, a little less of your money is working for you, and at the same time you are taking more risk—likely without ever really understanding it.

Some fixed-income funds that charge above-average management fees try to overcome that disadvantage by investing in riskier bonds with higher potential returns. But this additional risk can backfire, and you as the shareholder are the one who pays the price.

For five years from 2006 through 2010, the Oppenheimer Champion Fixed Income Fund (1.25 percent expense ratio) lost more than 20 percent annually. In that same five years, Vanguard's high-yield bond fund (0.28 percent expense ratio), which didn't invest in such risky securities, had a positive annual return of 6.3 percent. Which one of these operated in Wall Street's interests? Which operated in the shareholders' interests?

My second story involves sales goals that Wall Street imposes on brokers. Not long ago I met a young advisor who had just quit his job at one of the biggest investment firms in the country. He had thrown in the towel after deciding he was uncomfortable with the ethics of his firm. He had taken a job in the firm's Seattle branch office along with nine other greenhorns. When he finally left, he was the only one of his 10-person training group who was still there. No one in his class survived.

This young fellow was very open with me. He said that in order to remain on the payroll after the training period, he was required to produce commissions of at least $120,000 a year, or $10,000 a month. Even though the company knew he was only learning the ropes, he was encouraged to solicit business from his friends and family members. This is standard practice in the industry, and a young broker's friends and family may be his greatest asset to the company, since they are new prospects. Once he has obtained all the business he can from that source, he is less valuable unless he can excel at making successful cold calls.

To meet his production quota, this broker decided to focus on professional couples in their 30s and 40s who could save money for retirement in 401(k) accounts, individual retirement accounts (IRAs), and 529 college savings plans for their children. He immediately ran into two problems. First, he could not make any money if these professionals contributed to 401(k) plans because there was no commission. Second, if he could persuade them to invest in IRAs instead of their company retirement plans, the only products he could sell were load mutual funds and variable annuities.

This young broker didn't believe that his clients' best interests were served with either load funds or variable annuities. In addition, those products paid only about 5 percent in gross commissions. If he persuaded a couple to save $500 a month, his gross commission was $25. To generate $10,000 in commissions that way, he'd need at least 400 clients who were each adding $500 a month to their funds or annuities. That could take years, and he was under pressure to produce commissions now.

Then his company showed him a better way to meet his quota. It was better for him and better for his employer. But was this better for the investors? I'll tell you the facts and let you be the judge.

The company taught him how to sell variable universal life insurance and to pitch it as superior to 401(k) and IRA investments. He was taught how to explain the policy's tax-free growth of principal and the benefit in later years of being able to take money out tax free by borrowing from the policy, even before reaching age 59½.

He started making this sales pitch to clients, but he didn't fully disclose his motivation for his recommendation. Instead of making $25 on each month's $500 investment, his firm made 10 times that much because during the first year the insurance company paid the brokerage house $250 each month. That's right, a full 50 percent of the insurance premium.

Now our young broker could stay on the payroll by finding only 40 active clients instead of 400. Even better, if he could find investors who could write big checks immediately, for example $10,000 in a lump sum instead of paying monthly, the broker could make his quota by opening only a few accounts per month.

Over our third cup of coffee, he admitted that although the variable universal life insurance is a terrible solution for most clients, it's a wonderful solution for a young salesperson.

This chapter is about trust. If this man had been your broker, you would have liked him. I certainly did. You might easily have trusted him, as I did (of course without following any of his investment recommendations).

Brokers face constant pressure not only to sell but to sell high-profit products, which often turn out to be more risky. A friend of mine who is a broker told me his manager stopped by his cubicle one day to ask why he hadn't sold his allotment of a new security the firm was pushing. This broker, always direct and to the point, told the boss, "Because I think it's a piece of s___!" The manager replied, "You will either sell it to your clients or you will buy it in your own account."

You can certainly put your trust in Wall Street, and you'll be rewarded by the smiling faces and glitzy marketing materials designed to make you comfortable. But sooner or later, you will run smack into a conflict of interest. And in that conflict, Wall Street will win.

Main Street

Painting a picture of Main Street is more difficult, and that's just the problem. On Main Street, there are no reliable data, and you can't prove anything.

Informal contacts between individuals happen everywhere, all the time, in just about every conceivable manner. Short of organizations such as investment clubs (in which individuals share the work of doing research on individual stocks and then make group decisions to buy and sell), the communications on Main Street take place one interaction at a time. You sit next to somebody on an airplane. A neighbor remarks that she made $10,000 in the stock market last week; your brother-in-law claims to have special insights about some company or industry.

Main Street is a wonderful way to find out about restaurants, hotels, shops, dry cleaners, and hundreds of other products and services. People helping people really works in these realms, and the rise of review sites on the Internet has become a vast source of useful knowledge that reflects the experiences of real people.

But when it comes to investing, I don't think this works. When I choose a hotel or a restaurant, the stakes are relatively small. If I make a serious mistake, my evening or my vacation might be ruined, but not my financial future. On the other hand, when I decide how to invest my life savings, the stakes are very high. Casual just doesn't cut it.

Here are my main concerns. I don't know if somebody is telling me the truth. I don't know whether the success I'm hearing about was pure luck, or something else. I don't know how much risk this person is willing to take, or how much risk he or she actually took. I don't know whether this person's great success involved an entire portfolio or only a sliver of it. I don't know how much he or she knows about alternative choices that are available to me. I don't know how much, if anything, the person knows or cares about taxes, expenses, index funds, conflicts of interest, liquidity, and diversification. I don't know whether somebody with a huge portfolio acquired it by successful investing or by a big inheritance.

There's one thing I do know, however. It is very likely that I won't get the whole truth with documentation to let me confirm it.

I have talked to many investors who say they count on advice from friends and relatives whom they regard as more trustworthy than securities salespeople. Often, these investors turn to Main Street feeling very vulnerable after having lost money at the hands of a broker, who in fact may have been a clueless greenhorn or may have found this particular investor an "easy sale" for products that the company was eager to sell.

If you are following a guide from Main Street, you should know the answers to a few questions.

- Is my Main Street source telling me the truth—and the whole truth?
- Does he know how much risk I am willing to take and should take?
- Does he encourage me to practice smart diversification?
- Does he show me documentation to back up his stories of success?
- If he is indeed successful, why? Was it skill? Was it luck? Was it inside information?

- Does he have securities training or licenses?
- Does he have a long-term strategy that he can explain so I understand it?
- Does he have any legal obligation to me?

I don't think you are likely to get the whole truth from a friend or relative. Study after study has shown that most investors don't even know themselves exactly how their portfolios have performed. The human mind is very good at selective memory. We feel good when we remember our gains, and we find it quite convenient to forget our losses. I have a friend who likes to tell me of his market success. If I take him at his word, he has never had a losing trade. With a record like that, he should be managing billions of dollars for a mutual fund company!

Your neighbor may tell you how successful he is, but he won't tell you how much risk he's taken. Maybe that neighbor can afford to lose 50 percent of his investment portfolio. But when he actually sustains losses of that magnitude, does he regard it as a "normal" event to be expected? Will he tell you over the fence that he just lost half his money? Will he tell you he bailed out in panic after a big loss?

If you could see your neighbor's complete investment statements for 2008 and 2009, you'd have a pretty good idea. But I doubt you'll ever get that opportunity. And even if your neighbor can easily tolerate a huge loss like that, is that right for you?

If you listen carefully to what you hear on Main Street, you'll almost always find that the bragging is about short-term results, not those that span decades. Often, people ask me what I think the market is going to do this month or this year. A common question is some variation of: Where should my money be right now? I don't know the short-term prognosis for any investment. People who are focused on the short term are unlikely to succeed in the long term because they keep changing course instead of letting a good strategy work for many years.

Next time someone tells you about his great results, ask him to explain his long-term strategy and the assumptions that underlie it. You'll probably find him quickly changing the subject.

Most Main Street mavens don't believe much in diversification. After all, if you're super smart, you don't need to hedge your bets; instead, you'll tend to put everything on the winner. Many people will tell you quite confidently that there's no need to own more than 10 to 20 stocks in a portfolio. Their attitude is that diversification is for people who don't understand the market.

But in my view, the *lack* of diversification is for people who don't understand the market and for people who don't understand numbers, especially statistical probabilities.

This is one of the major differences between Main Street and University Street. Every piece of serious research I am aware of has concluded that investors need 100 or more stocks *in every asset class* to mitigate the risk of unexpected company failures. (Remember Enron, once highly respected and the seventh-largest public corporation in the United States.)

This means that if you invest in 10 great asset classes, as I recommend later in this book, you should have a thousand or more stocks. Does your Main Street guide tell you to do this? I'm guessing not.

Luck, Good and Bad

I've always been interested in the role that pure, dumb luck plays in investing. I remember a retiree who came into my office one day wanting my help in bailing herself out of a disastrous situation. Her first lucky day came in 1986, the year Microsoft stock went public. She bought 200 shares for about $11,000 and then hung on to them during Microsoft's glory days in the late 1980s and 1990s. The stock did so well, splitting time after time, that she stopped saving money. Microsoft was all she needed. Or so she believed.

This woman's second lucky day came in 1999, just a few months before the peak of the technology boom, when she sold all her Microsoft stock for about the same price per share she had paid originally, a bit more than $50. However, after eight splits, she owned more than 51,000 shares and had a capital gain of more than $2.6 million.

Lots of her friends naturally thought this woman was extremely smart and wanted to follow her next move, whatever it was. Some of them urged her to keep her winning streak going, and that certainly reflected the conventional wisdom in 1999.

But this woman had educated herself about investing, and she had heard one basic message loud and clear: diversify. That's what Bill Gates, Microsoft's founder and then the wealthiest man in the world, was doing. So she decided to diversify too.

Normally, diversification reduces risk. However, she had become addicted to winning, and she wanted to taste that grand success one more time. So she "diversified" by buying stock in 10 young, hard-charging technology companies that she knew were revolutionizing the world. Each one was another potential Microsoft. Surely she would strike it rich at least once more.

Remember what I said earlier about owning 10 asset classes and 100 or more stocks in each one? This woman believed that she was diversifying by owning only 10 stocks in a single asset class. By the end of 2002, all of her companies had shrunk to mere shadows of the promise they once held out to eager investors.

When she came to see us, this woman's portfolio was worth much less than the capital gains taxes she had paid on her Microsoft stock. Unfortunately, she and her family paid a huge price for the fact that she didn't understand proper diversification. Instead of living with a portfolio that could have supported them very comfortably forever, they had to live with the risk of running out of money and starting over.

Among investors who choose to place their trust in Main Street, this woman would be a star, somebody who was smart enough to turn $11,000 into more than $2.6 million with only two well-timed decisions. But anybody who had followed her lead in 1999 would have lost almost everything, as she did. You have no doubt heard that past performance does not indicate future performance, and as this story shows, Main Street is no exception.

Before you conclude that Main Street is trustworthy, remember there are a million reasons investors do what they do. Even when somebody else is successful, that doesn't mean his or her winning strategy is right for you. I know some investors who have tons of money and, therefore, look very successful. But if you look at their investment statements, you may find that they have extremely poor returns.

For some of them, that's just fine because they inherited more money than they'll ever need. Their net worth is wonderful, but it doesn't make their advice worthwhile. When I think of them I remember an old saying, sometimes told as a riddle, that packs a lot of truth into a few words: It is easy to make a small fortune; start with a large fortune.

Despite the success stories they will tell you, very few of the "experts" along Main Street have any formal understanding of how investing really works. This should not be surprising. Many very bright, hardworking people spend most of their time and much of their lives trying to figure out the markets. Some of them wind up on Wall Street, and others reside on University Street. That's where I would like to go next.

University Street

You might have an image of University Street as an ivory tower, removed from real life. There's probably some truth in this. Academics are not trying to make money from us and don't care very much what we think of them. In my mind, that makes them more trustworthy, not less. They are looking for the real truth, and that's what we investors should want. They have nothing to gain from us, hence no conflict of interest with us.

The national financial media certainly pay attention to the academic community. Morningstar, a heavily used and highly respected online publisher of information on stocks, funds, and exchange-traded funds (ETFs), was shaken up a few years ago when academic studies showed that its fund categories were relatively meaningless.

Equity funds, for example, used to be grouped in categories like capital appreciation, growth and income, and aggressive growth. But University Street found little correlation between those groupings and differences in performance. For example, two mutual funds that are being managed in hopes of achieving "aggressive growth" may hold very different portfolios. This plays right into one of the most important findings of the academic community. The overwhelming majority of any portfolio's performance can be accounted for by the types of assets in it.

Now Morningstar's nine-segment style box groups equity funds by the percentages of the portfolio in small-company (small-cap) stocks, large-company (large-cap) stocks, value stocks, and growth stocks. This information makes it easier for investors to put funds together into portfolios that take advantage of the valid research. And at the same time it removes some of the mystique of vague labels. (Quick: Do you know the difference between a growth fund and a capital appreciation fund?)

This is a good example of how solid research can move the investing process from intuitive to scientific. Academic studies cannot predict the future, but they can quantify the past in a way that's useful for identifying the sources of return and the sources of risk. If you want to be a successful long-term investor, you should want this type of analysis much more than the smiling faces in Wall Street ads and the unsubstantiated boasts you will find on Main Street.

Fortunately, you and I don't have to comprehend all the details of academic research in order to put it to work. Two famous professors, Eugene Fama and Kenneth French, demonstrated that three measurable factors can explain more than 90 percent of the difference between the return of any equity portfolio and the overall market. (Those factors are the size of the companies, the book-to-market ratio of the companies, and the volatility, or beta, of the stocks in the portfolio.)

You may wonder who keeps the academics honest. Unlike Wall Street, they aren't regulated by the government, and they aren't subject to the discipline of the marketplace. They don't have much reason to care whether or not we scoff at them or admire them.

What they *are* concerned about is the opinion of their peers. Peer review is a process in which professors evaluate the work of their colleagues, maintain standards, and try to protect credibility. Most academic papers are reviewed by experts in the subject matter before they are published. Papers that fall short may be critiqued in print or even denied publication.

This process isn't perfect, but it strongly discourages authors from making statements they cannot back up. To my mind, this is a comforting source of credibility.

Here's another important difference between Wall Street and University Street. Although most people have no interest in reading academic papers, those papers are available to anybody who wants to dig into them. On Wall Street, each firm acts as if it has a "secret sauce" or formula for getting results—and does its best to keep this sauce away from the competition. On Wall Street, if you share your firm's trade secrets, you are not only likely to be out of a job, you might even be taken to court. On University Street, you are rewarded for sharing what you know and having it critiqued by your peers.

Think of Wall Street as filled with know-it-all investors and managers who like to boast they have the best research, the best analysts, the best funds, the best resources of all kinds. Main Street is filled with people whose egos want us to believe they know it all, even though (as I have shown) it is pretty easy to find the limits of their knowledge and understanding.

Ironically, University Street is probably the smartest and best educated of these groups, yet academics make no pretense of knowing it all. For example, they recommend index funds that hold thousands of stocks, and they don't even try to pick ones that will be the winners.

When we're thinking about a recommendation of what to do with our life savings, we should ask: Where's the beef? Where's the evidence? Wall Street cleverly selects the evidence it will show us. Main Street almost never shows us the evidence. University Street is all about showing us that evidence.

This is why I think our trust should go to University Street. That's the door you should choose. Most of the rest of this book is about how we can apply the lessons of the academic community to become better investors.

In the next chapter we'll look into a basic issue that, in my own observations, trips up more investors than any other—the sometimes irresistible desire of investors and managers to beat the market.

4

WILL YOU TRY TO BEAT THE MARKET?

"The safe way to double your money is to fold it over and put it in your pocket."
—*Frank Hubbard*

I could make a case that this is the most important fork in the road for investors. If you take the wrong fork here—which in my view is trying to beat the market—you will be likely to make the wrong choices everywhere else. The chapter title poses a question, and your answer will affect everything else that you do.

Wall Street and Main Street, for different reasons, hope you will try to beat the market. I hope you won't.

Beating the Market Hurts

How does trying to beat the market hurt investors? If you are determined to beat the market:

- You will likely place much more trust in Wall Street and Main Street than is good for you.
- You will pay higher expenses and fees than are necessary.
- You will probably pay more taxes than are necessary.
- You will take more risk than is necessary to achieve the return you need.
- You will fail to diversify properly since you'll come to believe or even "know" that you have the market figured out (and you might start thinking that diversification is only for dummies).

- You will almost certainly spend more time fretting over your finances than you need to, and this anxiety will rob you of peace of mind.

- You may chase performance by investing in five-star funds at Morningstar, most of which have had average or below-average performance after they attain that rating.

- You'll have your eye on short-term trends rather than long-term returns.

- You'll find yourself susceptible to whims, fads, trends, and emotions.

- Because your focus will be on competition rather than on what you need, you'll have no idea when to stop, when you have reached the point that "enough is enough."

One very reliable way to beat the market, at least some of the time, is to put your money into a money-market fund or a bank certificate of deposit (CD). History shows that the stock market goes down approximately one day out of every three—and in about one of every three calendar years. If your money were in a money-market fund or a CD during those times, you wouldn't lose. You would beat the market.

Hundreds of times over my career, people have asked me: "Wouldn't I have been better off in CDs?" The answer is often yes. But it's not a useful answer because we can't invest retroactively. If you wanted CD returns, you could have taken your money to the bank at the start of whatever period you're asking about.

However, I can't recall anybody using the phrase "beat the market" to describe why they would invest in CDs or money-market funds. People who want to beat the market are hoping to make big money.

So what about you? Are you determined to go for it, or are you willing to accept the returns of the market? The first choice will put you on a roller-coaster ride with an unknowable landing. The second won't guarantee a smooth ride, but it's much more likely to provide an outcome you want.

How will you make this choice? I suspect your emotional makeup may play a bigger role than all the arguments and evidence I can give you. Neither you nor I nor anybody else can know the future, and it is theoretically possible that your market-beating efforts will lead to great success. But it's much more likely that those efforts will eventually lead you to give up after you have misused a lot of precious time and lost a lot of precious dollars.

That's the bad news. But there is good news, too. The good news is that you can be an above-average investor. If you are willing to do that, then you're in luck.

Becoming an Above-Average Investor

In theory, it should be easy. If you want to replicate the U.S. stock market as represented by the Standard & Poor's 500 Index, you have a choice of low-cost index funds and exchange-traded funds (ETFs). The same holds true for most major asset classes that I recommend. However, in real life, two things keep investors from achieving those returns.

The first thing that gets in the way of achieving market returns is Wall Street itself. Various expenses, fees, and inefficiencies are inevitable—at a very minimum somebody has to package an index, make it available to you, and keep records. This cumulative drag on your performance isn't always easy to see (this doesn't bother Wall Street very much), and it comes in many forms, including taxes that in some cases can be avoided or postponed.

One academic study of investor returns over a quarter century concluded that these factors reduced actual returns by about 2.5 percentage points. Some of this simply must be accepted. But every 0.1 percentage point of return that you keep or that you give up can add up to thousands of dollars over an investing lifetime. Savvy investors pay careful attention to the expenses they pay. They do their best to pay only for what is truly necessary or beneficial.

The second thing that gets in the way of achieving market returns is the behavior of investors. Because this behavior is within our control, the rest of this chapter is focused on this topic.

Investors trying to beat the market inevitably put their money into funds that have had recent hot performance. It's fairly easy to identify such funds, many of which have ratings of four or five stars at Morningstar. Financial media love to focus on five-star funds, and their audiences love to be introduced to gurus. Mutual fund companies love to advertise their five-star funds because they know investors feel most comfortable investing in something with good recent performance.

Morningstar denies that its fund rating system has any predictive value, and multiple studies have shown that in the years after a fund attains five-star status, such funds tend to have average performance at best. This inevitably creates disillusioned and disappointed investors, who often take their money out after a few years and put it back into *other* five-star funds.

If you could read the questions I get from investors, you'd see how difficult it can be to make sound decisions when you're worried about short-term trends and developments. Let me quote from a query that came in via e-mail while I was writing this book. It's from a 59-year-old woman (I'll call her Michele) who says her portfolio is 100 percent in equity funds, most of it in Vanguard index funds. She writes that she is pleased she has an average expense ratio of 0.14 percent, and I have to agree that is very favorable.

"Obviously, I know I should have a percentage of my portfolio in fixed income, and I was planning to do this in the past couple of years," Michele wrote. "But with the downturn in the market and lower interest rates, I did not want to sell stocks at lower values and worry about moving into bonds when interest rates were poised to rise."

Then come her questions: "What is your opinion? Should I wait for rates to rise and then buy into bonds? Should I make the switch gradually through dollar-cost-averaging? Or should I take some other course?"

Michele wants to do the right thing, but in my view she is asking the wrong questions. At 59, she's got an investment future that's likely to last 20 to 30 years, maybe more. I can't fault her for wanting to avoid buying bonds just before their prices could decline in response to higher interest rates.

But in focusing on these short-term concerns, Michele seems to be neglecting something much more important—her longer-term need to reduce the risk of owning a portfolio full of equities. And the best way to do that is by owning bond funds.

Michele obviously understands that. But she can't take the right action because she's so intent on getting her timing just right. Her biggest concern seems to be how to wind up with the most money in three to five years from now. Nobody can tell her how to do that. Maybe she'll do best if she shifts a big chunk of her portfolio into bond funds right away. It's also possible she will do better if she waits for a few years to see what happens. But that would not really solve her problem. Instead it would leave her with another question. When will she know the time is right to make the move? Unfortunately, she probably won't know until it's too late for her to take advantage of that "right time."

As you can see, it's easy to get tied up in knots over this issue. When we finally do act, it is often the result of emotions more than evidence and rationality.

Timing Decisions

Taken one by one, each of our timing decisions seems like the right thing to do at the time. But collectively, investors lose billions of dollars as they try to get into and out of the market at the right times. That's a startling statement, and I have evidence to back it up.

Although it doesn't seem logical, as a whole we investors get a lot less than the returns of the mutual funds in which we invest as we move money in and out of the market based on our fears, greed, and hunches about the short-term future.

For many years, a research firm in Boston named DALBAR, Inc. has published a study comparing the reported returns of mutual funds with the average returns of the shareholders in those funds. The firm's figures indicate that, during the 20 calendar years ending in December 2010, investors in U.S. equity funds achieved only 41.9 percent of the annualized return of the S&P 500 Index.

In those 20 years, the index had an annualized return of 9.1 percent, while the average equity fund investor's comparable return was only 3.8 percent. There are two reasons for this. The first is our in-and-out timing decisions. The second is that investors must pay in order to invest, and many of us pay far too much in expensive funds and sales commissions.

By the way, that means a lot of money was invested in ways that achieved far less than 3.8 percent. And as if this weren't bad enough, DALBAR characterized the figures as an improvement over the previous few years. And indeed it was. In the 20 calendar years ending in 2008, investors received only 22.4 percent of the return of the index.

You might think this is an anomaly, but academic studies have identified the same phenomenon.

These figures are so jarring that I believe it's worth your while to look at them in a little more detail. The lost performance happens because of the way investors pour money into funds and take it out. In short, after the market has been going up (read: "when prices are higher"), investors tend to pump more money into stock funds. And after the market has been going down (when prices are lower), investors tend to stop making new investments, and many even react by taking money out.

You could think of a mutual fund as having two pools of money. One is made of long-term "buy-and-hold" dollars that remain invested in spite of the ups and downs of the market. The second is "hot" money that investors put in and take out depending on fear, greed, and speculation.

Mutual funds report and advertise their performance as what happens to the long-term money (e.g., a dollar invested at the end of one year that is left there until the end of the following year). More often than not (remember, the market historically has gone up in two out of every three years), equity fund shareholders who left their money where it was were the winners. The losers were those who tried to second-guess the market.

Morningstar calculates what it calls "investor returns" for mutual funds, comparing them with the reported returns. (This information is available free at Morningstar's website.) Here's a hypothetical example. A mutual fund may have very good performance in the first quarter of a calendar year, gaining 8 percent from January through March, and then break even for the rest of the year. The fund's return for the whole year in that case would be about 8 percent. But if investors noticed the great first-quarter returns and started pouring money into the fund over the next several months, their substantial new investments would earn little if anything, and the fund's investor return would suffer.

Here's a real-life example from 2006. Fidelity's giant Magellan Fund (FMAGX) had a total return of 7.2 percent. The "investor return" in that fund, however, was only 4.9 percent. In other words, the collective investors in that fund actually achieved only about two-thirds of the return that they could have had by investing (or leaving) their money in the fund for the full year without additions or withdrawals.

Peter Lynch, who achieved legendary status during a long, successful run as Magellan's portfolio manager, once remarked that more than half the people who bought shares in the fund under his watch lost money because of their in-and-out timing.

Before leaving the Magellan example, it's interesting to think about why investors put their money in that fund to start with. I think it's mostly because they hope to beat the market through Fidelity's stock-picking and active management. How well did those investors succeed? To decide for yourself, think about this. In that same year of 2006, Vanguard's 500 Index Fund (VFINX) reported a total return of 15.6 percent. Morningstar calculated the fund's investor return as 15.3 percent.

To recap: The S&P 500 goes up 15.6 percent, and investors in Vanguard's index fund achieve 98 percent of that. In the same year Fidelity Magellan goes up 7.2 percent (so much for beating the market), and investors in Magellan collectively achieve only 68 percent of that—or less than one-third of the market return they were trying to beat.

So in this attempt to beat the market, not only did the actively managed fund fail, despite the efforts of the best managers and analysts at Fidelity, but investors in that fund failed to get even Magellan's return.

Christine Benz, personal finance director at Morningstar, has studied the effect of investor returns. She has found that the greatest discrepancies occur in the most volatile funds. Hot performance brings in money by the bucketload, but when the hot numbers turn cold, the money leaves just as rapidly.

The most infamous case I know of involves the CGM Focus Fund (CGMFX). In the summer of 2009, Benz looked at the reported returns and investor returns for CGM Focus, which had a risky, concentrated stock portfolio that had produced off-the-charts performance for years.

For three periods ending July 31, 2009, the following table shows the annualized fund returns and investor returns she found for CGM Focus.

As she pointed out at the time, "CGM Focus' trailing 10-year return suggests that a $10,000 investment a decade ago would now be worth $51,633. The fund's trailing 10-year investor return over that span, however, suggests that the same $10,000 shriveled to $1,585! The difference—all $50,048 worth—is attributable to investors' repeatedly mistiming their purchases and sales in chasing performance."

Period	Fund Return (annualized)	Investor Return (annualized)
Three years	down 3.75%	down 23.98%
Five years	up 8.83%	down 18.34%
Ten years	up 17.84%	down 16.82%

As this shows, investors can turn a mutual fund manager's modest loss into a huge loss. And they can turn a fund's superb 10-year performance into performance that can only be described as awful.

Unfortunately, this is not just a fluke.

Investor Behavior

DALBAR has been measuring the effects of investor behavior since 1994, focusing on collective decisions by investors to buy, sell, and switch mutual fund shares over short periods and long periods. Year after year, the firm has found that the average mutual fund investor earns less than the reported returns of mutual funds.

One key finding, stated in boldface type in DALBAR's 2011 report: "Investment results are more dependent on investor behavior than on fund performance. Mutual fund investors who hold on to their investments are more successful than those who time the market."

To conduct its study, DALBAR uses statistics showing mutual fund sales, redemptions, and exchanges every month to calculate "average" investor behavior. The methodology takes account of realized and unrealized capital gains and losses, dividends, interest, trading costs, sales charges, fees, expenses, and other costs that investors might pay.

I'm not a fan of active portfolio management, but many investors retain their hope that they have chosen managers who can beat the market. Yet those same investors second-guess that management by buying, selling, and making their own trading decisions.

As DALBAR's report states, "To take advantage of any alpha [essentially, additional return] created by portfolio management, investors need to remain invested and must not step in and out of the market."

Most investors think of themselves as in for the long haul. But even when they adopt carefully crafted long-term strategies, many of them don't stay in the game long enough to get the benefits. Instead, they react to the market, their feelings, and the nonstop commentary that has become a 24/7 staple of the financial media, undermining their strategies and their futures. According to DALBAR, in the past 20 years, the average holding period for equity mutual funds was 3.27 years. Let's see, that adds up to three years plus three months plus one week. Investors think this is the long term?

The phrase "staying in the game" makes me think of sports. Imagine a football team that walked off the field when things didn't work out quite as they had planned or expected. How much respect and sympathy would you have for that team?

Mutual fund portfolio managers "expend enormous efforts determining what investments to make, the right time to buy and the right time to sell" in order to increase returns by a few hundredths of 1 percent, the DALBAR report says, "only to see retail investors give up (entire) percentage points by poor timing of their buys and sells."

Here's another way you can think about this. It's common to report the annual return of a portfolio or a fund using four digits, two on either side of a decimal point. For example, Fidelity Magellan Fund's return in the year 2010 was 12.41 percent. In general, a portfolio manager changes the numbers to the right of the decimal point, the ones that make a relatively small difference. Investors, through their timing and stock picking, change the numbers to the left of the decimal point, the ones that make the big difference.

Investors routinely ignore the advice of the funds in which they invest to keep their money invested. Says DALBAR: "The result is that the alpha created by portfolio management is lost to the average investor, who generally abandons investments at inopportune times, often in response to bad news."

Here we are getting back to the behavioral finance territory we visited in Chapter 2, "Are We Our Own Worst Enemies?"

So how do we protect our portfolios from our personalities? The key may be to find ways to take a "time-out," a concept with which most parents will be familiar.

I'm not sure that a mandatory waiting period to buy and sell is a good idea. But if you can impose a voluntary waiting period on yourself, you'll be more likely to avoid falling into some common traps. If you have a strong urge to buy, sell, or exchange some investment, and if you're able to stop and think before acting, here are four questions to ask yourself.

- Do I believe that what I want to do will give me a significant benefit without any additional risk? (And if so, do I have evidence to support this belief?)
- Would I make this decision if I knew I had to live with it for 10 years before I could change it?

- What will this change mean to my level of diversification? Will I be getting rid of an important asset class? Will I be doubling up on other investments I already own?
- If I'm about to buy something, do I believe in it enough that if it lost 20 percent of its value I would want to buy more of it?

If you stop to ask yourself questions like these, you may be able to avoid having your emotions dictate your actions. And you may find it easier to resist the temptation to beat the market. I hope that's what happens for you.

5

HOW MUCH RISK
WILL YOU TAKE?

*"There are two times in a man's life when he should not
speculate: when he can't afford it, and when he can."*
—*Mark Twain*

If risk weren't a vital part of investing, you wouldn't need this book. We
might all be contented billionaires. Obviously, that's not the case. If you
want to be a savvy investor, the most important thing you can do is gain
a basic understanding of risks and how to successfully deal with them.

Throughout this book you will read anecdotes about investors who
ran into trouble in one way or another. Almost all that trouble involved
the risks they took. In fact, almost everything that can go wrong with
your investments involves the risks you choose to take with your money.
This is a choice you make whether or not you realize it at the time.

Most people aren't eager to think about risks. Wall Street certainly doesn't want us to focus on what can go wrong after we invest
our money. Look at the mutual fund and brokerage ads in any financial magazine, and you'll see photos of people who are happy to have
achieved their dreams. You'll never see ads showing people terrified to
discover they have lost their shirts.

At the urging of Wall Street, most investors concentrate on optimis-
tic thoughts and expectations. They dream of paying off the mortgage,
purchasing a vacation home, or buying a boat and riding off into the
sunset with time, energy, and money to do whatever they want.

However, I guarantee that when you make an investment that turns
out well, you won't suffer if you neglected to worry about how to handle
your success. On the other hand, if that investment fails to live up to
your dreams, you may wish you had paid more attention to the topic of
risk.

All forms of risk have one thing in common—the future is unknown and that certainly includes future investment results.

Some risk is objective, and some is emotional. To see the difference, imagine you are ready to invest $50,000 in a bank certificate of deposit (CD). You can buy one from your local bank or from a bank 2,000 miles away that is paying a higher interest rate. The objective risk is exactly the same in both cases. They are deposits guaranteed by the federal government. But the distant bank may entail more emotional risk because you can't walk into a branch and talk to a manager, and, in fact, you probably do not know anybody there.

But the distant bank pays more interest, and that extra money is the premium return you receive for taking a bit of extra emotional risk. Only you can decide if the extra return is worth the extra anxiety.

Let's start by examining objective risk, the kind that can be described in numbers.

The Real Nitty-Gritty

Most investors need to own some stocks for growth to at least keep up with inflation. And most investors need to own some bonds to add stability to their portfolios. As you know, stocks involve more risk and higher potential long-term return; bonds involve less risk and lower long-term return. How much should you have of each? Ah, that is the crucial question. Get that equation right and you'll be well on your way to mastering this topic.

Fortunately, you don't have to achieve military precision in dividing your portfolio between stocks and bonds. If your target is 50/50 and your portfolio is 52/48, you'll be fine. However, if your allocation strays to 60/40, you will be significantly out of balance. With 60 percent of your money exposed to the stock market instead of 50, you'll be taking more risk than you signed up for. This sort of change can happen easily, which is why I recommend rebalancing approximately once a year.

This chapter is not the ideal place to bring out detailed tables showing past losses and how they could have been avoided. This is important information, though, and you'll find it in Appendix B, "Fine-Tuning Your Asset Allocation," which I recommend highly. Appendix A, "Asset Allocation," outlines 10 methods you can use to help you find the amount of risk you should take.

Although I can't pinpoint the right level of risk for you, I can give you some helpful guidelines for finding that "sweet spot."

- Don't take too much risk. Investors often invest heavily in stocks, taking more risks as they seek higher returns. Far too often that leads to big losses that can be extremely difficult to recover. Remember this bit of math: if you lose 50 percent of your portfolio, it takes a 100 percent gain to get back to where you were. If your desire or need for return requires you to invest so heavily in stocks that you are beyond your comfort level, don't do it. It's never a good idea to ignore your emotions in order to chase higher returns. Instead, scale back your exposure to the stock market and find another way to achieve your objective. You can't achieve any return unless you stick with the program that produces that return—and you can't stick with a program if it scares you out of your pants and out of your investments.

- Don't take too little risk. You could avoid all the risks of the stock market by leaving your money in bond funds and cash. But there are two major problems with this. First, inflation will erode your purchasing power over time. This erosion is invisible but relentless. Second, interest rates always go up and down, and a change in either direction can hurt. Higher rates mean lower values for your existing bonds; lower rates mean less income when your bonds mature and you reinvest the proceeds.

- Strive for a moderate, balanced approach. In the long run, moderation will serve you better than either too much ambition or too much caution.

- If you're befuddled and don't know how to even start making an allocation choice, start with 50 percent equities and 50 percent bond funds. This might be too conservative, especially if you're young. It might be too aggressive, especially if you have barely enough money to meet your needs. If your equity allocation is within 10 percentage points of 50, in either direction, you are not likely to go too far astray. In the FundAdvice.com portfolio you will read about in Appendix G, "'Lazy Portfolios,'" I recommend 60 percent equities. On the other hand, many retirees get along very well with only 40 percent in equities.

- Once you have retired and started withdrawing money, find every way you can to keep the volatility of your portfolio low.

- Take time into consideration because you probably have different risk tolerances for different pools of money. Money you'll need in the next 12 months for a down payment on a house or college tuition should not be exposed to the stock market. Keep it in short-term bonds or a money-market fund. On the other hand, if your goal is achieving results in 5, 10, or 20 years, your risk tolerance may be considerably higher.

What Is Risk?

The American Heritage Dictionary defines *risk* as "the possibility of suffering harm or loss." Other definitions of risk use the words *danger, uncertainty,* and *hazard.*

Here's my own slightly modified definition of *risk*: a possibility, which you invite into your life, that you could lose something important. That something might be your physical safety, a relationship, or something financial.

This somewhat unorthodox definition makes it clear that risk isn't theoretical. It is about really losing something, and for the purposes of this book that something is money. Note also the word *invite*. Risk is not something imposed on you from the outside. At least in this context, it is something you choose, accept, and even encourage.

Obviously, nobody invests money in the hope of losing it. But investing is an area in which people get paid for taking risks, as we saw in the example of the distant bank offering a higher interest rate on CDs.

The lowest-risk investments such as Treasury bills, savings bonds, and money-market funds offer a narrow range of returns. The very best return you're likely to achieve and the worst return you will ever get are very similar: a modest profit. Investors take more risks because that modest profit isn't enough for them. If you take intelligent risks, not random ones, you may receive higher returns. This entire book is devoted to showing you how to do that, and what the payoff is.

One of the reasons so many people have so much trouble with risk is that investors don't get paid a premium return for doing what's easy and popular.

When you invest in stocks, even if you take my advice and diversify widely and wisely, you incur a lot more risk than keeping your money in the bank. But over the long run, the rewards have been much greater from stocks than from bank deposits. Higher risk goes along with higher expected returns.

Measuring Risk

Objective risk involves the part of the brain that thinks. It can be measured in volatility, the risk that the value of an investment will fluctuate in wide swings, sometimes very quickly. This can be unsettling at best, and it can lead to unfortunate decisions.

Volatility is most often tracked with a statistic known as standard deviation. If you want to know how this is calculated, you can find that easily on the Internet. For our purposes, what you need to know is that a higher standard deviation indicates more volatility, hence less stability, less certainty—and more risk.

Here's why that is so: If you own a stock with a price that stays within a narrow range, you are likely to feel more comfortable than if the price goes up and down like a yo-yo.

Usually, bonds have lower standard deviations than stocks. That makes them less risky. You can take advantage of this by making sure that some part of your portfolio is invested in bond funds in order to dampen the higher volatility of the stock funds you probably want to own. You can think of this as mixing cold water with hot water to achieve a comfortable temperature.

In statistical terms, your goal as an investor should be to get that temperature just right in order to either (1) achieve the highest return you can while you keep the risk level tolerable or (2) find the lowest-risk way to achieve the return that you need in order to accomplish your goals. The first stance is usually more appropriate for younger investors. The latter one is usually more appropriate for older investors—or investors of any age who have more than enough money.

The upshot of this is that whenever you're evaluating past and potential future investment results, you should want to know about returns but also about standard deviation. In Appendix C, "The Ultimate Buy-and-Hold Strategy," we use those two numbers to evaluate every change we make as we gradually put together the right asset allocation.

It's easy to start with a basic portfolio and make changes that will increase the expected return. But it's tougher to do what we did in that appendix, increase the return without increasing the level of risk as measured by standard deviation. When you can do both those things at once, using data spanning decades of experience, you have found something special.

Wall Street would like us to believe that there are investments that combine high expected returns and low risks. Millions of investors have lost billions of dollars trying in vain to find that combination. However, the fundamental equation remains—risk and return can't escape each other.

If you still hope that there's a genuine exception to the rule and there's an investment with high returns and low risk, think about what would happen in that case. The news about such a miraculous investment would spread like wildfire on Wall Street. Lots of money would rush into this investment, demand would overwhelm supply, the price would go up—and that higher price would drive down the return. All this would probably happen before you ever heard about it, and certainly before your broker could call you and tell you about the opportunity. This is how capitalism works.

Specific Risks

Before we leave the topic of objective risk, I'd like to briefly mention some of the specific risks that investors face. First, a few major risks faced by investors in bonds.

- *Default risk* is the danger that the corporation or government agency that issued the bond might be unable to pay interest and/or principal when due.
- *Interest rate risk* is the risk that interest rates will rise, making the bonds in your portfolio worth less than they were because investors can buy new bonds that pay more.
- *Reinvestment risk* is the danger that, if interest rates fall and your bonds mature, you may have to reinvest the proceeds at a lower interest rate.

Stock investors are exposed to many risks too, of course.

- *Stock risk* is similar to default risk for bonds. The company behind a stock can fail and become worthless. Enron and

Washington Mutual Bank are two classic examples from recent years.

- *Stock selection risk* is the danger that you, a broker, or a fund manager picks a group of stocks that turn out to be dogs for one reason or another. In the early part of the 20th century, there were dozens of automobile companies based in the United States. Only three survived. In the early days when personal computers were mainly of interest to geeky hobbyists, there were many brands. Only one of those early entries achieved great and lasting success, and the others are forgotten. The lone survivor, named for a popular fruit, now has almost as much stock market capitalization as Microsoft and Intel combined.

- *Market risk* can apply no matter what stocks you own. If the whole market drops, your portfolio will probably drop too because investors will be soured on the whole idea of investing.

- *Inflation risk* is the very real danger that the money you save or earn will lose some of its purchasing power. Anybody who depends on fixed-income sources such as pensions and long-term bonds is exposed to this risk. Even at a very modest rate of 3 percent annually, inflation can be a huge problem. You might retire on a fixed income of $50,000, more than adequate for your needs. But if your cost of living goes up 3 percent, after 25 years, you'll need $104,700 to replace that purchasing power.

- *Asset risk* is the danger that you remain invested in the wrong asset class for a prolonged period. For example, there was a 10-year period when the S&P 500 Index lost 1 percent per year while other asset classes were profitable.

- *Tax risk* can't be eliminated for most investors, and your investment gains will be diminished by income or capital gains taxes. You can mitigate this risk by reducing your trading and by choosing mutual funds with low turnover rates and high tax efficiency. And, of course, it usually makes sense to take full advantage of tax-sheltered accounts such as 401(k)s and similar plans, as well as individual retirement accounts (IRAs).

- *Expense risk* is triggered when unnecessary expenses erode your returns. Expenses are like anchors being dragged behind a sailboat. They may be invisible, but they inevitably reduce the speed of the boat.

- *Event risk* is the danger that some unexpected event or series of events will topple investment markets. A few well-known examples are Pearl Harbor; September 11, 2001; and the 2011 earthquake in Japan. Unless you keep all your money in government-backed savings accounts, there's no absolute protection from sudden events like that. One of the things we should do, if only to maintain our sanity, is to remember that life is uncertain; in fact, that is part of what makes life worth living.

- *Fraud risk* is the danger you'll fall victim to somebody's dishonest effort to take advantage of you. This is different from making dumb decisions. Fraud deliberately creates victims. To keep from becoming one of those victims, deal with reputable investment professionals, be very skeptical of deals that look too good to be true, and take the time to check out unusual opportunities before you plunge into them. If somebody tells you the only way to take advantage of some deal is to make a decision immediately, there is only one correct answer: "I'll pass."

The Solution

Part of the solution to all these kinds of risks is diversification, the topic of Chapter 6, "How Will You Diversify Your Investment Holdings?" If you own bonds issued by only one company and that company fails, you may be out of luck. If you own a bond fund with dozens or hundreds of issuers represented in its portfolio, a single failure won't bring down the ship. The same is true of stocks. Own only a few and you are making huge bets on your selection. Own hundreds or thousands indirectly through mutual funds, and your returns won't hinge on what happens to a few choices.

Emotional and Psychological Risks

We now get to the type of risk that involves the part of the brain that feels and reacts instead of thinks and evaluates. Even though this can't be measured, it's very real. When you lose money—or you're afraid of losing money—that takes an emotional toll on you and affects the decisions you make. University Street cannot help much with this type of risk because it's subjective. It changes and varies a lot from person to person.

No matter how hard I try to prepare investors for the uncomfortable times of loss, when the market heads downward, many well-crafted investment plans are abandoned. I recall talking to a couple a few years ago. They fell into a trap by planning for risk in terms of percentages, but when they experienced actual losses, they reacted in terms of dollars.

They had opened an account with about $1 million, and after extensive discussion they agreed they wanted enough of their portfolio invested in stock funds that they would be exposed to the risk of losing up to 15 percent at some point. They had invested at a time when the market was heading upward, and they made some profits before the market—and their portfolio—hit a serious pothole.

They called me one day, upset that from the peak they had lost about 7 percent of their retirement funds. When I pointed out that this loss was well within the range they had accepted a few months earlier, the husband angrily reminded me he had lost more than $80,000. "I could have bought a very nice new car for that," he said. His wife told me they could have bought a college education for their grandson with that money. And now it was gone.

"I gave you this money to protect it," the husband said. Even after I pointed out that their investments had held up better than if they had left that money where it was previously invested—and after I showed them that they had done better than the market as a whole—they remained deeply distressed.

They did stick with their portfolio, and they eventually achieved some good investment gains. But they reminded me that no matter how much we think we understand and accept the possibility of loss, the real world is not the same as the theoretical world.

Real people experience real losses in real time, and there is no way to avoid it.

When things are going well, we want to take more risk. If the sun is out, we are happy to forget about the raincoats and umbrellas, even if thunderstorms are in the forecast. When things are going badly, we want to take less risk. When it's raining cats and dogs, even if sunshine is forecast, you may feel very silly packing the beach towels and sunscreen.

Here's another useful way to think about this. When the market has been doing very well and everybody seems to be making money, it's easy to invest. Emotional risk is low. Yet this is the very time that financial risk is high. That's because stock prices are cyclical, and the higher you get on the upward curve, the closer you are to the inevitable point when the curve starts downward.

Conversely, when the market has been doing poorly, fear is much stronger than greed. When prices have been sliding for a long time, you probably won't feel like keeping your money in the market, to say nothing of adding more. At this time in the market cycle, when emotional risk is high, financial risk is relatively low.

In practical terms, this means that if you follow your emotions to get in and out of the market, your behavior will be counterproductive. When investors are emotionally affected by the ups and downs of the market, they lose their objectivity and become susceptible to fear and greed. The best investors have the resources, patience, and perspective to do the opposite of what the masses are doing.

So what's the answer? I think the answer is moderation. Trying to get rich quick can be very dangerous. Giving up too easily is also dangerous.

I believe the best defense against the various kinds of risk is to have and follow a sound plan that, as much as possible, operates on automatic pilot without requiring you to constantly make decisions. The second-best defense may be having somebody you trust, whether it's a spouse or a professional advisor, who will slow you down when you're eager to do something that may be the wrong thing for you.

Risk Never Ends

Dealing with risk is a never-ending job. It's not normal to see month after month of market gains without setbacks along the way. What's surprising to me is how many investors seem surprised when those setbacks occur. The stock market's ups and downs are normal. Any market that goes only one way for any prolonged period is abnormal and should be treated with suspicion.

Timeless Truths About Risk

The best way to deal with psychological risk is to learn and understand the most important time-tested truths about risk. Here are six things that I hope you will keep in mind.

1. Markets are unpredictable, and there is no evidence that anybody can consistently make accurate short-term forecasts. Most of the predictions made one year ago were so wide of the mark that they turned out to be worthless.

2. Over the past 200 years, the world's stock markets have had a long-term upward trend, and I believe that trend is likely to continue. Capitalism appears to be gaining strength in the world, not losing it.

3. There is no risk in the past. We always know what we should have done, and we know how things turned out. It's easy to look back and believe that things developed in an obvious manner. But it's impossible to see the future with that sort of clarity.

4. The market's immediate response to good news and bad news is almost always exaggerated. At times, many investors seem to believe that the entire future is wrapped up in the headlines of the day. The best way to cope with short-term problems and uncertainties is to ignore them as much as you can.

5. The market rewards perspective and patience. (See Chapter 11, "The Perfect Investor," for more on this.)

6. No investment approach works best every single year.

Are You Taking Too Much Emotional Risk?

It can sometimes be challenging to know whether you have taken on too much risk. So here's a simple risk-evaluation test you can take by asking yourself three questions.

-   Have you lost any sleep over your investments?
-   Do you feel compelled to watch the financial news and check fund prices daily or weekly? (We are talking about feeling compelled, not just curious.)
-   Does the financial news make you worry about your future?

If your answer to one or more of those questions is affirmative, you may have taken on too much risk. In that case, you should find somebody who can help you sort through the financial and emotional issues that are causing stress in your life.

You can hire professionals to allocate your assets, rebalance periodically, minimize your taxes and expenses, and perform most of the other tasks that make up good investment practice. But you are the one who must deal with the emotional side of risk. Nobody else is in charge of that, and this is a job you can't delegate.

Here is something I wrote to our clients in 1998 and again in 2000, two years when fear suddenly reared its ugly head in the minds of many investors:

> In the very good times, it seems as if investing is about accepting wealth. You put down your money, almost like planting it in a garden, and watch it grow. But in fact, in good times and bad, investing is really about *managing risk* and *managing your emotions*. If you want to be a successful investor, you've got to do at least a decent job at both those tasks.
>
> If you can do those two things, you're well on your way to success.

That idea is just as valid and valuable now as it was in 1998 and 2000.

6

HOW WILL YOU DIVERSIFY YOUR INVESTMENT HOLDINGS?

"In theory, there is no difference between theory and practice. In practice, there is."
—*Yogi Berra*

Diversification isn't an inherently gripping story. I know that some people want to roll their eyes when they come to details that I find fascinating.

In a nutshell, here's why I hope you'll read this chapter instead of skipping it. The academics on University Street have found time after time that the choice of asset classes in your portfolio makes much more difference to your long-term returns than anything else you do.

This isn't really a strange idea, if you think about it. Imagine you are a cook making a stew. It's reasonable to believe your choice of ingredients for that stew, and the quantities you use for each one, will have a profound effect on the success of that stew.

You can't put just any old things in a pot and expect a great stew. Likewise, you can't put just anything into a portfolio and expect to make a lot of money. Great chefs choose great ingredients and mix them carefully. In this chapter I'll show you how to choose great assets and how to mix them in just the right way in your portfolio. As you'll see, there's a huge potential payoff for getting this right.

Thick textbooks have been written on this topic, known as asset allocation, and I have good news for you: You don't have to read them. I'll give you the essentials and show you how to put them to work for you. In my previous book *Live It Up Without Outliving Your Money!*, this topic took six chapters. Here, it gets just one, plus Appendix C, "The Ultimate Buy-and-Hold Strategy."

Despite my strong views, you don't have to do it my way. You have a choice. Many investors take the easy way out by refusing to dig into the details that we'll cover here and assuming that one or two mutual funds are all they need.

When you're making a stew, you can grab whatever ingredients are handy and throw something together. Your family will be fed, and if the outcome is mediocre, tomorrow is always another day. Likewise, when you wash your car, being lazy is not likely to have life-altering consequences.

But when you are managing your life savings, a mediocre outcome lasts a lot longer—possibly forever. The consequences can change your life. If you or your heirs will need your money someday in the future, you can't afford to be lazy about this.

From Chapter 5, "How Much Risk Will You Take?" you should realize the importance of properly dividing your portfolio between stocks and bonds to control your risk and potential return. Now it's time to look at the details of the stocks you should have in your portfolio.

Lazy investors can get by with a mix of only three well-chosen mutual funds: one that owns U.S. stocks, one that owns international stocks, and one that owns bonds. Some investors even leave out international equities—and I'll show you why that's a big mistake.

However, for only a little extra time and effort, you can take advantage of the many decades of investment results that make it clear there is a huge advantage when you own small-company stocks and value stocks in addition to the large-company growth stocks that dominate so many people's investments. In addition, foreign stocks now make up more than half the world's total market capitalization. I'll show you that investors can reduce their risk and often increase their returns by including companies based outside the United States.

To follow this discussion, you should understand the phrase "asset class." Think of this as a group of stocks that share common characteristics that can be identified and measured—and that have some demonstrable effect on risks and returns. This last requirement means that "stocks of companies headquartered in Minnesota" is not an asset class, but "stocks of companies headquartered in the United States with price-to-earnings ratios of 15 or more" could be one.

When Small Is Beautiful

In the 1970s, Roger Ibbotson, professor of finance at Yale School of Management, and Rex Sinquefield, co-founder of Dimensional Fund Advisors and its co-chairman until he retired in 2005, published a book on historical stock market returns that identified a relationship between various asset classes along with their risks and returns going back to 1926.

One thing they quickly discovered was a pronounced difference between the returns of stocks of small companies and those of large companies. Over many years and many periods, they found that small-company stocks (e.g., the Microsoft of 1986) outperformed large-company stocks (e.g., the Microsoft of 2011). The reason is not hard to find, and Microsoft gives us a familiar example.

The Microsoft of 1986, the year when its stock was first available to the public, was much riskier than the huge, relatively mature Microsoft of today. Back then, computer software was an industry with great growth potential, but nobody knew which of the leading companies of the early 1980s would prevail. Now, except for Microsoft, those software companies are all but forgotten.

Bill Gates, Microsoft co-founder and arguably one of the brightest people of his generation, understood the risks of his company. When Microsoft moved its operations to what was then a suburban forest near Seattle, he insisted that the first buildings be designed so they could be useful to another business in case his whole venture failed.

Why should you invest in small companies? That's a good question, and here's the simple answer. Taken one at a time, small young companies are extremely risky. But if you buy enough of them, you'll pick up those that grow to become the giants of tomorrow. As an asset class, these stocks often pay off handsomely for investors who can take the risks.

Thanks to the work of University Street and to indexes that track thousands of stocks, we can see some impressive long-term effects. Over a 50-year period, an index of the smallest 20 percent of publicly traded U.S. stocks compounded at a rate of 12.4 percent annually, compared with 9.8 percent for the Standard & Poor's 500 Index, which is made up of the largest stocks. If you invested $100,000 and earn 9.8 percent (S&P 500) for 30 years, you'd have $1,652,228. If instead you earned 12.4 percent (small stock index), you'd have $3,334,182. The companies were smaller, but your nest egg was a lot bigger.

Let's make something clear right away: I'm not recommending you put all your money, or even the majority of it, into small-company stocks. That would be too risky. But if you put some of your money into hundreds or even thousands of small-company stocks, you'll most likely be glad you did. Using the return figures I just cited, if you split your money 50/50 between large-company stocks and small-company stocks, you would likely improve your return over the S&P 500 Index. You would be benefiting from what University Street calls "the size effect."

When Value Is Valuable

There's a second extremely important "effect" that University Street measured for many decades and then quantified and explained. It's the "value effect." Its message is counterintuitive: Stocks that most investors don't want tend to be better performers than stocks that most investors do want.

Value stocks, as they are called, are ones with low prices relative to their underlying sales, profits, and other accounting values. There's always a reason, maybe valid and maybe not, that these stocks are in the dumps. They are risky, and University Street has discovered that owning them by the thousands is a good way to make money. That's the short version of this discussion.

This information may be hard to believe at first, and so let's dig into it in a nontechnical way to explain why it holds up.

The companies behind some value stocks are in dying industries or unglamorous businesses such as railroads, electric utilities, or garbage disposal. Some have awful products or management. Some may have just gone through a string of losses. For whatever reason, their prospects don't look very bright, and investors don't want to pay high prices for them.

For reasons you know from our discussion in Chapter 2, "Are We Our Own Worst Enemies?," investors often overreact to bad news, selling out-of-favor companies in such volume that their prices can drop to levels that make them bargains. However, there's always this very interesting question: When is a cheap stock a bargain, and when is it just a dog?

The Gannet Company

You may not be familiar with the name of the Gannett Company, but you have undoubtedly seen (if not purchased) its main product. Gannett is the largest publisher of newspapers in the United States, leading an industry that for much of the 20th century was extremely profitable. In the 1970s, Gannett was a darling of Wall Street, essentially a chain of dozens of local monopoly newspapers that could set their advertising rates to whatever level was necessary to produce the profits that headquarters demanded.

In the early 1980s, Gannett made a bold and expensive move by creating *USA Today,* the first truly national newspaper, using satellite technology and the overnight capacity of its own and other printing plants across the country to facilitate early morning delivery. The company invested heavily in distinctive newspaper boxes and made sure the new paper was available everywhere for travelers.

USA Today proved to be a great success, but society was changing. Starting in the 1990s, the newspaper industry ran into problems it couldn't totally solve. Advertisers had new ways to reach customers. Newspaper readers had hundreds of new ways to spend their time and get information and entertainment, including cable television, VCRs, music videos, personal computers, video games, and, of course, the Internet. Today, the newspaper business is trying to figure out its future in a world where owning printing presses and fleets of delivery trucks is no longer a ticket to success.

When I started thinking about Gannett for this discussion, I was pretty certain that it must be a value stock. Fortunately, I could easily go to Morningstar.com (http://www.morningstar.com/) and confirm my suspicions by looking at just one number—the company's price-to-book ratio. For Gannett, that number is 1.8.

That number means that investors are willing to pay only 1.8 times the money they could theoretically obtain if Gannett shut down its business and sold off all its assets. By contrast, Microsoft's price-to-book ratio is 4.5. This means investors think Microsoft's business is worth a lot more than its physical assets. Apple's ratio is 5.8, indicating a very high level of confidence in that company's future.

The price-to-book ratio for the stock market as a whole goes up and down over time, and a single number doesn't mean very much. But University Street has taught us that price-to-book is a reliable way to objectively determine what's a value stock at any given time and what isn't. You can find some details in Appendix C, "The Ultimate Buy-and-Hold Strategy." For now, just keep in mind that there's a quantitative way to identify thousands of stocks as value stocks. And conveniently for individual investors, we can invest in mutual funds that track indexes of value stocks. I do that; you should too.

You and most other investors would probably much rather fill your portfolios with stocks like Apple than stocks like Gannett. So why am I telling you to buy some of the market's dogs? The reason is easy to understand and, for many people, maddeningly difficult to accept emotionally. Investors make money buying stocks that not everybody wants and selling stocks that are in high demand. Many decades of stock market experience and many academic studies have concluded that investors reap better long-term returns if they include such value stocks in their portfolios.

(And remember, again from Chapter 2, "Are We Our Own Worst Enemies?," we don't always know as much as we think we do, especially about the future. Just as investors collectively might be underestimating the comeback power of Gannett, they might also be overestimating Apple's ability to keep churning out high-end, high-demand consumer products.)

In the 50 years from 1961 through 2010, an index of U.S. large-company *growth* stocks like today's Apple and Microsoft grew at an annualized rate of 8.9 percent, while an index of U.S. large-company *value* stocks like Gannett grew at 11.4 percent.

In real life, that difference in return is enormous. If you are approaching retirement, it is not unreasonable to expect that you will have money invested for 30 years. Here's the math: At 8.9 percent per year (large-company growth stocks), a $1,000 investment over a 30-year period would grow to $12,907. At 11.4 percent (large-company value stocks), $1,000 would grow to $25,501.

The value effect works with small-company stocks, too. In the 50 years from 1961 through 2010, a U.S. small-company growth stock index grew at a rate of 8.2 percent, while an index of U.S. small-company value stocks grew at 15.3 percent. For $1,000 invested over 30 years, that's the difference between $10,637 and $71,594.

Now we've covered two main factors that drive long-term growth in the price of stocks: size and what could be described as valuation.

And here's the bottom line—your long-term stock returns are likely to be higher if you tilt your holdings a bit toward small companies and toward value companies.

When choosing the types of stocks to hold in your portfolio, you have a choice. Will you take the lazy, comfortable approach by investing only in large-company growth funds? Or will you ask your money to work harder for you and take the less comfortable route of including some index funds that specialize in small companies and value companies? I hope you'll take the latter route instead of the former.

One way to do this, as you will see in the sample portfolios in Appendix E, "Mutual Fund Model Portfolios," and Appendix F, "Getting the Most from the 50 Largest Employer Retirement Plans," is to have half your equity holdings in growth and half in value, half in large and half in small. How can you have four halves? This is a miracle of modern mathematics that's easy to understand if you think about a deck of playing cards. It's possible to hold a stack of cards in which half are red and half are black, half have values of more than seven and half have values of less than seven. One stack of cards, four halves—amazing, but true.

Going Global with International Stocks

Once you accept the fact that diversification is good and you make the choice to include value stocks and small-company stocks, it takes almost no extra work to invest outside the United States as well. Think of this as putting the world to work for you.

U.S.-based companies represent less than half the world's total stock market value. I recommend you have half your equity investments in companies headquartered outside the United States. And while you're at it, make sure this international part of your portfolio includes small-company stocks as well as large-company stocks, value stocks as well as growth stocks. Investing internationally won't necessarily bring you higher returns. But it will reduce your risk by smoothing out the peaks and valleys of the market as U.S. and international stocks don't always go up and down at the same times and the same speed.

In addition to large, small, growth, and value, I recommend including a slice of emerging markets stocks in your portfolio. Emerging markets represent one of the best ways I know to invest in assets that have demonstrated they can provide premium returns at reasonable levels of risk.

Emerging markets represent the great growth potential of young economies like Brazil, Chile, Poland, Hungary, and Russia. Once this category included China, a country that is now truly "emerging" to become a great world economic power. The average age of the population in emerging markets countries is lower than that of most developed countries. As these younger populations mature, millions of people will become new stock investors and begin thinking about retirement. This will raise the demand for stocks in their countries, and that will raise prices.

Stock markets in these countries have the potential to experience the type of success we saw in the United States in the 1990s. You can participate in that, quite easily, by owning one or more mutual funds that invest in those economies. For various reasons that I consider legitimate, emerging markets funds charge higher expenses than you will have to pay elsewhere. But I believe the potential reward is worth the expense.

As much as I believe in emerging markets, it's important to remember that while they may be the frosting, they are not the cake. Therefore, limit emerging markets to no more than 10 percent of the equity part of your portfolio.

If this discussion seems to be entering uncomfortable territory, I'm not surprised. Investors around the world shy away from stocks and markets that are outside their comfort zones. In Canada, one prevalent concept of international diversification is to divide an equity portfolio in thirds: Canadian stocks, U.S. stocks, and stocks based in other countries. You can find similar patterns in many places, including Germany, Australia, Great Britain, and Japan.

Yes, Japan. Remember our discussion of how humans tend to be overconfident and think we know more than we actually do? Well, that's not limited to North America. In the 1980s it was obvious that Japan's economy was taking over the world; the future looked extremely bright. Japanese investors can be forgiven for thinking all they really needed were stocks of Japanese companies.

But the bottom fell out of the Japanese economy and the Japanese stock market, and that country has been struggling ever since to recover. The huge earthquake in March 2011 was a major setback to that recovery. Japanese investors who once staked everything on what to them were domestic companies lived to regret it. Those who diversified outside their country, even when that may have seemed stupid, eventually were glad that they did.

Even if international stocks don't increase the long-term return of a portfolio, the additional stability they bring is especially valuable to retirees withdrawing money from their investments. In fact, as we will see, international stocks can make the difference between a retirement portfolio that lasts a lifetime and one that runs out of money prematurely.

Let's take a look at some evidence, based on stock market returns for the 41-year period from 1970 through 2010. Here are three variations of a properly diversified portfolio; the only difference among them is how much they held in international stocks.

- All equity, 0 percent international: annual return 11.2 percent
- All equity, 25 percent international: annual return 11.9 percent
- All equity, 50 percent international: annual return 12.6 percent

What those numbers don't show is risk. The all-equity portfolio with half its assets in international funds had a 26 percent higher return than the S&P 500 Index—and at less risk. That much difference in return is extremely significant to almost any investor. To obtain that much additional return with less risk is truly a game-changing combination.

At the end of this chapter I'll show you the real-world effect that this can have on you as an investor. But first here's one additional asset class to add to my recommendations.

Real Estate Is More than Where You Live

In any retirement portfolio that is sheltered from taxes, you should include real estate. I'm not talking about your home. I'm talking about commercial real estate, which includes office buildings, parking lots, shopping malls, theaters, apartment complexes, hospitals, and other real estate that makes money. It's easy to invest in commercial real estate through mutual funds that own real estate investment trusts (REITs).

The main point of owning commercial real estate in your portfolio is not to increase your returns, although sometimes it will do that. The point is to improve your portfolio's diversification and decrease its overall volatility. If you pay any attention to business, you know that commercial real estate has its boom times (lots of construction cranes poking into the sky) and its bust times ("For Lease" signs everywhere).

As an investor you can put these business cycles to work to your benefit because REITs and the broad U.S. stock market typically move up and down out of synch with each other. That combination reduces the volatility of a portfolio, which in turn makes it easier for investors to stay the course.

The suggested portfolios in the appendixes include real estate funds, both in the United States and internationally. Real estate funds fit well inside tax-sheltered accounts such as individual retirement accounts (IRAs) and 401(k) plans. But for two major reasons, you may not want to own them in taxable accounts. First, REITs are required to pay out most of their profits to their shareholders in the form of dividends (instead of, for example, using profits to buy more real estate). Those distributed profits are taxable in the year that investors get them. Second, REIT dividends don't get the favorable tax treatment that is given to corporate dividends, so they are taxable at your top rate.

Is Diversification Worth It?

I realize I've covered a lot of ground in these few pages. You could very easily put all your equity dollars in a U.S. large-company mutual fund and be done with it. You'd have a decent long-term return without having to think about small, value, real estate, international, and emerging markets. There's no question that diversification takes a bit of extra work. But the payoff for this additional work is so significant that it can literally change your life.

The best evidence that I have consists of historical investment returns for the 41 years from 1970 through the end of 2010. This period included three major bear markets, three strong recoveries, and a bull market that lasted for much of the 1990s. It included a decade of very high interest rates followed by a period when interest rates fell to nearly zero. I don't know whether or not the future will be anything like the past four decades, but those 41 years encompassed a very diverse market and economic period.

Any investment mix that held up well during all that turmoil deserves consideration as a worthy long-term strategy.

For those 41 years, the S&P 500 Index compounded at a rate of 10 percent per year. That's a very respectable long-term return. But it was left in the dust by an all-equity portfolio that was diversified as I recommend, with small-company, value, real estate, and international stocks. That portfolio grew at an annual rate of 12.6 percent.

You might think all that diversification added risk, but just the opposite was true. The standard deviation of the S&P 500 Index was 15.7 percent vs. 15.3 percent for the diversified portfolio.

Annual percentage returns are just numbers, of course. But let me show you what a difference those 2.6 percentage points could make to a real-life investor. Many people retire with $1 million in investments and a life expectancy of 30 years. So let's apply these returns to that.

Over 30 years at a rate of 10 percent annually, $1 million would grow to $17,449,402. That's mighty impressive . . . at least until you calculate the result for a growth rate of 12.6 percent: $35,168,327. Some people would say this is an example of the "magic" of compound interest: A 26 percent boost in annual return doubles the long-term return. That's true, but in my mind the real "magic" in these numbers comes from diversification. Not only is the return doubled, the risk goes down.

Of course I know that very few retirees will actually have 100 percent of their portfolios in stocks. I have repeatedly held up the notion of a 60 percent equity portfolio as a reasonable option for many people. So let's look at the numbers for a 60/40 split, with and without diversification.

In the period 1970–2010, a portfolio made up 60 percent of the S&P 500 and 40 percent in five-year U.S. Treasury notes—in other words a portfolio without the diversification I have described—grew at a rate of 9.5 percent a year. When the equity side of that portfolio was diversified as I recommend, that annual return was 11.7 percent.

Applied to a $1 million portfolio for 30 years, the portfolio with only the S&P 500 in equities would grow to $15,345,909; the one with diversified equities would grow to $27,942,162.

Your results won't be the same as these, naturally. I can't even promise that full diversification will outperform the S&P 500 Index in the future. But now you have a basic understanding of why you're likely to get better results by combining all these asset classes and putting them to work for you. For a more complete discussion of these diversification steps, read Appendix C, "The Ultimate Buy-and-Hold Strategy."

When all is said and done, the evidence for diversification is so compelling that this should be an easy choice. Depending on how much money and how much time you have, this choice could be worth $1 million to you—or even more.

7

HOW WILL YOU PROTECT YOURSELF FROM YOURSELF?

"With self-discipline, almost anything is possible."
—*Theodore Roosevelt*

Even if you have the best long-term plan in the world, coupled with the best investment strategy in the world, your plan and your strategy aren't worth much if they don't get executed, or if you let the financial news and your own emotions derail your plans.

As we have seen, emotion-based decisions almost always hurt investors in the long run, even if they bring short-term comfort. Moving in and out of the market is a huge trap, sometimes encouraged by Wall Street (because trading is a huge source of revenue) and Main Street (because your neighbor may obtain an emotional reward by getting you excited or upset about something).

You may know what you should do, but if you wait until you feel like doing it . . . well, if you have ever tried to be serious about dieting or exercising, you know what's likely to happen! Fortunately, the solution is relatively simple, easy, and cheap if not free. The answer is to set everything on automatic as much as possible: savings, rebalancing, withdrawals, and more.

If you have a job or collect Social Security or a pension, you probably have income automatically deposited into your retirement savings or a bank account. If you have a mortgage, you very likely have signed up for automatic payments, an arrangement that ensures that your payments are made on time.

Automatic Savings

The most basic investing task is saving money. Almost everyone you know would probably rather have you spend money than save money. Buy a shiny new boat, and you'll have lots of admirers who would love to go for a ride. But if instead you add $10,000 into your savings, how big a crowd do you think you'll attract? Almost every business you come into contact with would like you to spend money instead of save it. Many of those businesses will even loan you the money to spend!

In this environment, saving isn't always easy. If you wait until you're sure you don't have some other use or need for that money, saving may never happen.

Fortunately, it's easy to save money automatically. The company 401(k) is the perfect example, with three benefits.

- It makes savings automatic, so you don't have to do anything to make it happen.
- It uses dollar-cost-averaging to help you automatically buy more shares when prices are low and fewer shares when prices are high.
- It gives you a tax deduction, letting you put more money to work for you than if you saved after-tax dollars.

In addition, virtually all banks and credit unions can arrange automatic transfers from your checking account to a savings account. If you own a mutual fund, whether inside an individual retirement account (IRA) or a taxable account, you can probably set up an automatic investment plan, often known as an AIP. Here's a case in which you can take advantage of Wall Street's insatiable desire to manage more of your money.

The habit of automatic savings is one you should establish as early in life as you can. Whatever percentage of your income you can set aside—10 percent of the gross is a good target—should regularly be transferred to savings or investments without requiring any active decision from you. Soon you will get used to doing without this part of your income, just as you probably do with the taxes and other deductions that come out of your paycheck. If you're not doing this already, it's never too late to start.

Spending less than you take in—in other words, living below your means—is a habit that will serve you well throughout your life. It will let you build cash reserves and an investment portfolio on which to retire. Making the decision once, and putting your savings plan on automatic, is a welcome case where "the easy way" produces better results than the hard way.

Automatic Stock Selection

University Street recommends using index funds, and I wholeheartedly agree for a number of reasons. When you own an index fund, you automatically keep up to date with the individual stocks in an asset class, for example, the Standard & Poor's 500 Index.

When a young, fast-growing company is becoming more and more important in its asset class, an index fund automatically makes sure you own more of it. And when a company is gradually dying or swiftly imploding, as Enron did a few years ago, an index fund automatically reduces your exposure to it.

Automatic Rebalancing

Rebalancing is the periodic chore that involves shifting your investments from one asset class to another in order to keep your overall risk in line with your needs. It's a fundamental step in managing your portfolio.

Here's a simple example of why it's necessary. Let's assume you want to keep 60 percent of your portfolio in stock funds and 40 percent in bond funds. You've determined that is the right mix of potential returns and potential risk for you. Then a big bull market comes along and your stock funds do very well. After a year or so, stock funds make up 75 percent of your portfolio.

That's good, right? Yes and no. It certainly is good that you made that money. But now your portfolio has more exposure to risk than you determined is right for you. To bring your portfolio back in line with your target risk level, you should sell some of the stock funds (take some profits, in other words) and use the proceeds to buy more of the lower-risk bond funds. This is rebalancing.

To do this right, you should evaluate every asset class in which you're invested, rebalancing large-company stocks with small-company stocks, U.S. stocks with international stocks, value stocks with growth stocks, and so on.

There are a couple of ways to avoid having to figure it all out by hand. I think the best way to rebalance your investments automatically is to have your financial advisor look at your account once a year and make the necessary trades without intervention from you. If this is done within a taxable account, the sales may result in tax consequences, so you may want your advisor to help you weigh the benefits against the costs.

A second way to rebalance your investments automatically is to invest in a mutual fund that does this internally. Some "moderate allocation" funds like Vanguard Balanced Index Fund normally try to keep around 60 percent of their portfolios in stocks and the rest in bond funds and cash. These funds are constantly buying and selling securities as money comes in and goes out, and the trades can be managed in order to maintain the proper asset balance.

Third, if your funds are within a single fund family such as Vanguard, you can call that company once a year and ask them to calculate and make the trades to bring you back into balance with your targets.

If you're regularly adding money to your portfolio, you may be able to maintain the proper balance by directing your new investments to asset classes that are below their percentage targets. That is a very good way to do it. However, this won't be very effective if your portfolio is much larger than your contributions.

Likewise, if you're regularly withdrawing money, you can select the funds from which you take money in order to preserve the right balance.

If none of these solutions works for you, I suggest you make rebalancing at least semi-automatic by scheduling yourself to do it once a year. If necessary, set aside a certain day or weekend every year to get this done. Or make a date with a friend, or perhaps your spouse, to get it accomplished together. However you do it, be sure to rebalance your accounts!

Automatic Withdrawals from Your Portfolio

Eventually, we reach the point in our investing careers when it's time for our portfolios to pay us, instead of the other way around. If you have to decide every month how much you're going to withdraw for living expenses, you'll spend a lot of time and energy that most likely could be put to much better use. And you might end up having constant conversations with your spouse or partner; one of you is likely to want to spend more and the other less.

Those discussions may never go away completely, but you may be able to limit them to one per year. Each January (actually you can choose any month for the start of your personal financial year) evaluate your portfolio and your needs for the coming 12 months. This is the time to have the discussion with whomever is appropriate in your situation. Make your decision; then set up automatic monthly transfers into your checking account.

Early in this chapter, I identified the problem as emotion-based decisions, and I said the answer is to set everything on automatic. As shown, doing this is not mechanically difficult. However, it may be emotionally hard because you are effectively relegating your feelings to the backseat. Leaving our feelings out of the investment equation is relatively easy for some of us and pretty hard for others. That's the way we are wired as human beings.

However you do it, when your finances are on automatic pilot, your decisions can become lasting policies instead of one-time turning points. My suggestions in this chapter should let you experience less anxiety and more peace of mind. I believe that's a win-win financial prescription.

8

THE BEST

"We investors as a group get precisely what we don't pay
for. So if we pay nothing, we get everything."
—*John Bogle*

It's always risky to prescribe the best of anything. "Bestness" can't be proved objectively unless everybody has agreed in advance to the terms—and that would take much of the fun out of it. However, after nearly half a century of studying the investment business, and being in it for much of that time, I think I've earned the right to have some opinions about what's best for investors. This chapter is a sampler of those opinions.

Perhaps the most important article I've ever written is called "The Ultimate Buy-and-Hold Strategy," first published in the 1990s and updated online every year since then. As I mentioned in that article, I never use the word *ultimate* lightly. It means the very best that I know.

The 2011 version of this article is reproduced in Appendix C, "The Ultimate Buy-and-Hold Strategy," with permission of Merriman, Inc. This "ultimate" strategy hasn't changed much in the past 15 years, although it has been fine-tuned as new tools and new insights have become available.

When I started thinking about this chapter, I realized that I'm always looking for better ways to help people be successful investors. The landscape is constantly evolving, and even though my list isn't the final word on the subject, I hope you will regard this chapter as a sort of travel guide to some of the best attractions in the world of investing.

The Four Best Investment Books

Education and experience should be the basis of most of our efforts in life, so I'll start with the best four investment books I know.

Mutual Funds for Dummies

Eric Tyson's book is a must-read for any serious investor. The author has written five national bestselling personal finance books and is the only author ever to have four books simultaneously on *Business Week*'s business book bestseller list. You should think of your investment portfolio as a family business that you will manage and depend on the rest of your life. When a business is that important, you should understand how it works and how to take care of it. This book is a vital business manual, a guide to the inner workings of the funds that are likely to make up the bulk of your retirement portfolio. If you learn and apply what's here, you will avoid mistakes that cost other investors hundreds of thousands, if not millions, of dollars. I think the meatiest part of this book is the section called "How Mutual Funds Work and Should Work for You."

The Little Book of Common Sense Investing

John Bogle is the founder of Vanguard and the inventor of index funds designed for individual investors. He's a classy, intelligent, and articulate guy. He's part of Wall Street, yet he's still on our side. The subtitle of his book, *The Only Way to Guarantee Your Fair Share of Stock Market Returns*, is a clue to his topic: index funds. You can pick any mutual fund in existence today and be nearly certain that he has had an impact on how that fund's managers operate. His work has kept the pressure on mutual fund families to reduce their fees and expenses. While his own fund family offers some actively managed mutual funds, Bogle has shown that investors don't need active managers. He's a tireless fan of diversification, a voice of truth, and an enemy of expensive, misleading financial advertising.

Bogle's background is extremely impressive, and I'd love to give him the full introduction he deserves. But right now I'm recommending the book, not the man, so I'll let you find out on your own about his business background and his magna cum laude graduation from Princeton plus the many awards and accolades he has won.

The Little Book of Common Sense Investing summarizes and condenses many practical lessons that we can put into practice. This book is a quick read that's worth coming back to from time to time.

Your Money and Your Brain

Jason Zweig does an outstanding job of showing how the invisible hard wiring inside our brains dictates a lot of our behavior—often to our detriment. Though I managed to hit a few of the high spots of the book in an earlier chapter, there's much more in this fascinating look at the psychology of investing. I have read this book at least five times, and each time I learn more about how easily and stealthily our fear, happiness, greed, risk, surprise, and regret can hijack the thinking part of our brains. Zweig is a columnist for the *Wall Street Journal* and was formerly a senior writer at *Money Magazine* and mutual funds editor at *Forbes*.

Live It Up Without Outliving Your Money!

Published in 2008, my previous book covers some important territory that I have had to leave out of this book. Even though the investment returns I cited in that book are a bit out of date by now, I would not change the basic messages a bit. The book starts by describing some very common mistakes investors make and how to avoid them. There's a short chapter that profiles two people I have known for many years (names have been changed to protect the innocent and the guilty), one of whom has done essentially everything right and the other of whom has done essentially everything wrong. I've learned from them both, and you can too.

Much of *Live It Up Without Outliving Your Money!* is devoted to asset allocation and retirement distributions in more detail than I can present them here. Toward the end of the book is a chapter on finding good professional help and another one that describes my personal long-term estate plan. If you're thinking of leaving some assets to your family or your favorite charities, that chapter alone is worth more than the price of this book. I don't recommend that you copy my plan, but I recommend you think "outside of the box" as I did before you cast your own plans in stone.

The Best Mutual Fund Families

There are many fine families of mutual funds, and I'm going to slight some of them by describing only two: Vanguard and Dimensional Fund

Advisors. I believe that almost all investors can get what they need from these two sources. As Garrison Keillor says in his "A Prairie Home Companion" radio spots for Ralph's Pretty Good Grocery, "If you can't find it at Ralph's, you can probably get along without it."

In my mind, the ideal fund family offers a broad range of choices of no-load index funds or passively managed asset-class funds with low expenses, low portfolio turnover, high tax efficiency, and few barriers to entry such as huge minimum initial investment requirements or long restrictive holding periods.

For do-it-yourself investors, Vanguard is the winner, hands down. Vanguard sets a very high standard, forcing its competitors to shave the expenses they charge shareholders. Vanguard has a wide selection of index funds as well as some excellent offerings that use conservative, low-cost active management.

Vanguard is strong in international funds, small-cap funds, value funds, and many varieties of fixed-income funds. It also has a good lineup of target-date retirement funds that provide easy solutions for some people. I wish Vanguard had funds covering a few important niches such as international small-cap value, emerging markets small cap, and emerging markets value. But those asset classes are not essential, and their absence is not enough to drive me away from Vanguard. In sum, I think that Vanguard is the "Ralph's Pretty Good Grocery" of mutual fund families.

Vanguard's big competitor is Fidelity. For more than 15 years, we have been recommending portfolios of Fidelity funds and portfolios of Vanguard funds. Our recommendations are carefully tracked by the *Hulbert Financial Digest*. The best all-equity portfolio we've been able to construct at Vanguard has outperformed our Fidelity all-equity portfolio by 1.8 percentage points annually. Our moderate 60 percent equity/40 percent fixed-income Vanguard portfolio has outperformed our similar Fidelity portfolio by 1.4 percentage points a year. There's no mystery about the reasons for these differences, which can make an enormous impact on a portfolio over a lifetime. They result from Vanguard's combination of lower fees, lower turnover, more index funds, and the advantage of passive vs. active management.

If you use the services of an independent advisor, Dimensional Fund Advisors is miles ahead of all its competition. These funds are available through about 1,500 advisory firms in the United States, Canada, and Australia. Compared with Vanguard, Dimensional offers more asset classes, lower turnover, lower expenses in some cases, and more "oomph" in some important equity asset classes. For example, Dimensional value funds dig deeper into value stocks, and its small-cap fund portfolios have smaller average capitalization. In plain English, that means that when you want value and small, you get more of each from Dimensional funds than from Vanguard funds.

Dimensional funds aren't exactly index funds, although their expenses and turnover are very low. The company uses state-of-the-art portfolio design and trading techniques that have historically led to superior performance when compared with index funds in comparable asset classes. (See Appendix D, "The Best Mutual Funds," for a more detailed discussion of this.) This fund family was started in 1981 and manages more than $180 billion in assets.

From its start, Dimensional has been guided by the findings of two of the most distinguished academics of the past 50 years. Dr. Eugene Fama, currently Robert R. McCormick Distinguished Service Professor of Finance at the University of Chicago Booth School of Business, rocked the financial world when his Ph.D. thesis was published in 1965 in the *Journal of Business*. Dr. Fama concluded that stock price movements are unpredictable and essentially random. He is often regarded as the father of the efficient market hypothesis, which has shaped the thinking of most market analysts ever since he published it in 1970.

Dr. Kenneth French is the Carl E. and Catherine M. Heidt Professor of Finance at the Tuck School of Business, Dartmouth College. He has previously been on the faculties of MIT, Yale, and the University of Chicago. He is a former president of the American Finance Association and a research associate at the National Bureau of Economic Research. At Dimensional, Dr. French is on the board of directors, chairman of the investment policy committee, and director of investment strategy.

The Best One-Fund Portfolio for Life

This is a really tough call because there is no single mutual fund that does the whole job. Still, some people are determined to have the ultimate in simplicity, and I hear this question often. Although no answer I could give is even close to perfect, I think the exercise is useful because it forces me to determine what the most important things are.

So let me take you through my thought process when I absolutely have to recommend only one mutual fund that could not ever be changed (i.e., one fund for life). My first requirement would be finding a balance between potential growth and control of risk. That requires a fund with equities and bonds; this is commonly known as a balanced fund. Second, I would want low expenses, low turnover, no sales load, and relatively high tax efficiency (although that matters less if this fund were in an IRA or a similar account). This tells me I should look for an index fund, and I already know that Vanguard is the place to look for those.

If that were all I needed, I could settle for the Vanguard Balanced Index Fund. But less than 1 percent of that fund's portfolio is invested in international stocks and very little in mid-cap and small-cap stocks—all assets that investors should own for the long haul.

After looking at every Vanguard fund, my choice has to be the Vanguard STAR Fund. Knowing this fund's ticker symbol, VGSTX, lets you look it up easily at Morningstar.com (http://www.morningstar.com/) and other financial websites.

This no-load fund has more than $14 billion in assets and charges expenses of 0.34 percent, which is reasonable though not rock-bottom. The fund's overall allocation is approximately 60 percent stocks, 35 percent bonds, and 5 percent cash. This is close to the traditional pension fund model for long-term growth and stability, and it makes sense for many people's long-term needs.

I'd prefer a lower annual portfolio turnover rate, but STAR's 22 percent is not bad. More than 20 percent of its assets are international stocks. And while I'd prefer a bigger dose of small-cap stock holdings, requiring a single fund (in this case a fund of funds) to do everything well is a tall order. In the 10 years ending May 31, 2011, this fund had a compound annual return of 5.3 percent. That's respectable for a very turbulent decade and considerably more than many investors achieved. However, STAR is certainly not a risk-free fund. Its value dropped by 9.9 percent in 2002 and by 25.1 percent in 2008.

The Best Two-Fund Portfolio for Life

This is still a very challenging assignment, but at least it lets me choose separate equity and fixed-income funds. My equity choice is Vanguard Global Equity Fund (VHGEX), which has a higher-than-average weighting to value stocks (a plus) and an above-average 57 percent of its portfolio in international stocks. That is more exposure outside the United States than many people find comfortable, but it accurately reflects the global markets and all the opportunities they present.

Investors in this fund should understand that during the times when U.S. stocks are doing better than international ones, this fund's performance will lag behind some of the competition. With its big international stake, this fund's annual expense ratio of 0.44 percent looks like a bargain. The fund's 64 percent annual turnover rate is higher than I would prefer, but once again I can't get quite everything I want in a single package.

In the 10 years ended May 30, 2011, this fund's annual return was 7.4 percent, much better than the results of the U.S. large-cap stock indexes. However, this fund carries the risks inherent in any all-equity fund. In 2008, it lost 46.7 percent—well beyond the tolerance of most investors. For that reason, it's essential to combine this fund with one that holds bonds.

The fixed-income part of this two-fund portfolio belongs to Vanguard Total Bond Market Index Fund (VBMFX), a huge intermediate-term bond fund with expenses of just 0.22 percent.

The advantage of having two funds in a simple portfolio is that you can vary the percentages in each one to adjust your overall level of risk. When you're trying to determine that risk level, you'll get some good guidance from Appendix A, "Asset Allocation," and Appendix B, "Fine-Tuning Your Asset Allocation."

For an investor who wants to set-it-and-forget-it for life, I'd be inclined to put 50 to 60 percent of this portfolio in the equity fund and the rest in the bond fund. Bolder investors might want 70 percent in equities, while more conservative investors might scale the equity fund down to 40 percent of the portfolio. I think most people will be well served staying within those ranges. Whatever your needs, these two funds make it possible to get the allocation right.

The Best Target-Date Retirement Fund

Every target-date retirement fund is built on two assumptions. First, you want all decisions made inside a single investment package that does everything. Second, you can identify a "target date" when you'll retire and start taking money out for living expenses.

Most target funds include both stocks and bonds and become more conservative as the target date (e.g., the year 2035) approaches. Investors in these funds almost always sacrifice some return they could have from some important asset classes such as small-cap stocks, international stocks, and value stocks.

Still, investors who are willing to make that sacrifice will be relieved of the tasks of rebalancing, choosing a level of risk, and periodically adjusting that level as they grow older.

Before reaching for your checkbook, take the time to recognize that target-date funds are not as simple as they seem. If you're thinking of putting money in one, do two things. First, determine the fund manager's plan for the portfolio when the target date is reached. (Will everything suddenly go into bond funds? Will the fund continue to own a significant allocation in equities?) Second, use the information in Appendix A, "Asset Allocation," to determine how much risk is right for you, and choose a target year on that basis instead of merely designating a year when you want to retire.

Picking the best of this breed is relatively simple. Almost all academics agree that expenses are a huge determinate of future rates of return. If you concur, then you should look no further than Vanguard, where expenses are substantially lower than the competition. Pick a fund that fits your expected retirement date (e.g., Vanguard Target Retirement 2035), and you're set. Vanguard says the 0.19 percent expense ratio for its 2035 fund is 61 percent lower than the average of other funds with similar portfolios.

The Best Source of Information on Mutual Funds

Often the first place I go for reliable information on funds is Morning star.com. I don't buy into Morningstar's star rating system nor the fund-picking recommendations of the company's lineup of talented analysts and commentators. But you'll find lots of interesting articles there. And when I want the facts on a fund, this is where I can find them.

To see how much is available, visit this site, find the Funds tab, and punch in the ticker symbol for Vanguard's STAR fund, VGSTX. If you click on the tabs for such things as Performance, Portfolio, Expense, Tax, and Ratings and Risk, you'll find that Morningstar truly lets you look "under the hood."

When I'm studying a fund at Morningstar, I usually look for 6 to 10 pieces of information, depending on what I'm trying to learn. To illustrate, I'll take you through some of the items I found when comparing two emerging markets funds, Templeton Developing Markets (TEDMX) and Vanguard Emerging Markets Stock Index (VEIEX).

The following table shows the data points for TEDMX and VEIEX.

Even if you didn't know anything more about these funds than those statistics, you could paint a comparative picture. Templeton has much higher expenses and turnover, two important drags on performance. It also has fewer stocks, which increases risk.

I'd like to digress for a moment to note something about the 13.8 percent TEDMX return. Yes, it's the return reported by Morningstar. It's officially correct, and this is the standard way that Wall Street reports the performance of load funds. But I think this practice is just plain misleading because it ignores the 5.75 percent upfront sales load. In effect, it treats that load as if the disappearance of 5.75 percent of an investor's money is irrelevant. This makes for a very unfair comparison with no-load funds.

Let's clarify this point with a simple hypothetical example. Suppose you invest $1,000 each in two funds that have identical performance and leave your money there for one year. Let's say each fund's reported return is 10 percent and that the only difference between these two funds is that one involves a 5.75 percent front-end sales load and the

	TEDMX	VEIEX
Expense ratio	1.9%	0.35%
Sales load	5.75%	zero
Portfolio turnover	46.8%	12%
Assets	$3 billion	$57 billion
Most recent 10-year performance	13.8%	15.4% (about equal to the difference in expenses)
10-year return lost to taxes	1.01%	0.15%
Number of stocks in portfolio	72	869

other has no load. If you looked only at the stated return, you would conclude that after one year your account value would be the same in each fund: $1,100. But in fact, the 10 percent return of the load fund applied only to the $942.50 that was invested in the fund's portfolio. That means your account in the load fund would be worth only $1,036.75. The figures for returns would have you believe that $1,100 is equal to $1,036.75. But, of course, you know that's not true.

Unfortunately the effect of that load gets worse. Assume that your account in each fund grew an additional 10 percent in the second year. The no-load account would then be worth $1,210, compared with only $1,140.43 in the load fund. That difference, $69.57, is now equal to nearly 7 percent of your original investment. You may have heard the phrase "the gift that keeps on giving." This growing expense could be called "the cost that keeps on costing."

When you take that sales load into account, I find it hard to see how anybody could make a credible case for buying the Templeton fund instead of the Vanguard one.

OK, back to Morningstar.com. In addition to fund data, this site has lots of interesting tools and calculators, which you can find by clicking on the Tools tab toward the top of the page. With the mutual fund screener tool, you can choose from a long list of criteria and let the site find funds that have what you're looking for. You can do it over and over again until you find exactly what you want.

Morningstar's Instant X-Ray tool is also worth mentioning. It might be particularly helpful if you have acquired lots of stocks and funds over the years. For each of your holdings, you will be asked to enter the amount (either in shares or in dollars) and the ticker symbol. When you have done that, this tool will give you a picture of your whole portfolio as if it were just one mutual fund. If you think you are well diversified just because you own lots of funds, Instant X-Ray can set you straight pretty quickly by showing how much of your money is concentrated in a limited number of stocks and asset classes.

The Best Asset Class to Own in the Future

Don't misunderstand me here. Owning just one asset class is not the right approach for any investor. However, I will use this category as a way to point out a frequently overlooked asset class that deserves to be in the portfolios of most long-term investors: small-cap value stocks— both United States and international.

You know from Chapter 6, "How Will You Diversify Your Investment Holdings?" why University Street favors small-cap stocks and value stocks. Over the decades, small-company stocks have had better long-term returns than large-company stocks, which are much more widely known. Likewise, value stocks have had better long-term returns than growth stocks, the appeal of which is easier to understand. And as we saw earlier, along with higher returns, small-cap stocks and value stocks involve higher risks.

I'm not saying you should put the majority of your money into small-cap value stocks. But I am saying you should be sure that at least some of your money is invested that way.

How do you do it? If you work with an advisor and have access to Dimensional funds, it's easy. Dimensional has a U.S. small-value fund, an international small-value fund, and even an emerging markets small-value fund.

If you're an investor at Vanguard, you can use the Vanguard Small-Cap Value Index Fund (VISV) for U.S. small-value stocks. Vanguard does not have an international small-value fund, but you can use a brokerage account to buy the WisdomTree International Small-Cap Dividend Fund (DLS), an exchange-traded fund (ETF).

The Best Investment Strategy

This one is easy, and yet it's impossible at the same time, a conundrum. The best strategy for you is the one that produces the best return that you can and will actually achieve. Lots of strategies and lots of mutual funds produce dazzling returns on paper. But if they are so volatile that you sell out when the going gets tough, then you don't get that performance.

What really counts is the return that you actually get as an investor. Remember our discussion in Chapter 4, "Will You Try to Beat the Market?" of the DALBAR study and the CGM Focus Fund. The fund had spectacular returns over the course of years, but actual investors lost money. As we saw, that wasn't the fund's fault. The reason for the difference was investors' buying and selling decisions.

So the best strategy for you is the one you will actually carry out, the one that keeps you within your comfort zone by limiting the amount of risk you take. I've discussed this in the two previous chapters, and you'll find some alternative ideas in Appendix A, "Asset Allocation."

Your best strategy is one that's set up to work automatically without costing you peace of mind or a good night's sleep. Getting just the right combination will take some work, and I believe you may profit from the help of a good advisor. I use the word *profit* with a full understanding of what that word means. An advisor's help will cost you something; think of that cost as an investment. If you get really good advice and put it to use in your portfolio, I believe you'll have a good shot at saving or earning $5, $10, or maybe even more, for every dollar you pay for that advice. That's my idea of a profitable investment.

The Best Source of Investment Advice

Advice has to involve more than good ideas. It has to be based on knowledge of you and your individual situation. In my view you can't do better than working with a well-educated, independent advisor who has a fiduciary responsibility to you. (In Appendix I, "Hiring an Investment Advisor," you'll learn how to find such a person.) Your advisor should understand your risk tolerance, your need for return, and any beliefs or emotions you have that could trigger you to make hasty decisions that you may regret later.

I don't think you can get that level of advice online, even from the most sophisticated calculators that ask penetrating questions and tap into awesome computing power to find answers. Nevertheless, the Vanguard and T. Rowe Price websites have lots of good calculators, studies, and thoughtful articles, all of which are easy to access. They will give you ballpark answers that you can take to an advisor for further discussion.

If you like numbers and want to roll up your sleeves a bit with detailed online retirement planning, you may want to check out Henry K. "Bud" Hebeler's site, Analyzenow.com (http://www.analyzenow .com/). You may not be familiar with that name, but this site gets more than a million hits a year. His free retirement software program has a sterling reputation, and *Consumer Reports* has named Analyzenow.com one of the best retirement-planning sites.

I've known Hebeler since the 1980s, and I know how much he cares about helping people. Although his site is not fancy, it goes well beyond the basics. He is a serious guy with an impressive professional background.

After graduating from the Massachusetts Institute of Technology (MIT), from which he has three degrees, Hebeler took a job as an engineer at Boeing, working his way through financial analysis, procurement, sales, and corporate long-range planning until he became president of Boeing Aerospace Company. Now retired, he focuses on disseminating sound financial planning information to individuals, companies, government agencies, and other organizations.

The Best Financial Writer

At the risk of sounding like a broken record, I'm giving this nod to Jason Zweig at the *Wall Street Journal*. The financial media are filled with material from many distinguished writers, and I'm pleased to personally know quite a few of them. They are all under pressure to keep coming up with fresh, provocative angles in order to keep their audiences coming back for more.

We've all seen the lists of the top 10 cities in which to retire. Have you ever wondered why the best cities are different every year? Have these cities changed radically since the last list was published? I'm sure not. No, this year's list has to be fresh. The same is true for lists of the best funds, the best managers, the best stocks, the best of everything.

This pressure to keep reinventing the truth can make it hard for journalists to just call them as they see them. However, in my view Zweig comes as close as anybody in the media to telling the truth about what's likely to work for investors. His thorough understanding of emotional and psychological factors sets him apart from most of his peers. You can subscribe to the *Wall Street Journal* to read him, but it's also easy to find his articles online. I recommend you do so.

The Best Person to Predict the Future

This must seem like an odd category for me to include since I don't believe in predictions. But no matter how many times I deny having any knowledge of the future, some people just won't give up thinking that I do, and that they can somehow coax this mysterious knowledge out of me.

Human nature all but demands that we try to predict the outcome of almost any event. Some of us believe or pretend that we know the future, and even make bets that we are right. In the short term, that's gambling—on the horse or team that will win the race or the numbers that will come up in Reno or our state lottery.

Some gamblers eventually bankrupt their families because they think they know much more than they actually do. Lots of commentators and pundits make a living making predictions about the short-term behavior of the markets and other things they can't possibly know. They're always ready with new predictions when the older ones don't pan out.

Perhaps the most blatant example is that of the people who name the date, and even the exact time, when the world will end. When that time becomes history and we're still here, they can usually figure out a new date.

I believe that anybody who regularly makes public financial predictions is probably doing so for marketing purposes, ego satisfaction, or some other reason that has little to do with trying to help you or me.

All this is a long-winded way of saying that I can't name a reliable guru. However, if I had to place my bet on the best predictors of the future, I would have to give the nod to the team of Dr. Fama and Dr. French, identified earlier in our discussion of the best mutual fund family.

These two professors developed the three-factor model that influences the way trillions of dollars are invested. I've covered their key beliefs elsewhere in this book—in the long term, small-cap stocks will outperform large-cap ones and value stocks will outperform growth stocks. These predictions seemed revolutionary when they were new, but now they seem much more mainstream because they have been so widely accepted.

There's another very important thing they predict. It's quite possible that over the next 30 years just the opposite will happen, that large-cap stocks and growth stocks will outperform small-cap and value stocks, respectively. When Dr. Fama was asked how his theories could be wrong for so many years, he had a ready answer: "You're not very patient, are you?"

The Best Bet to Beat Buffett

My answer to this one may surprise you.

Benjamin Graham was a leading economist and Columbia Business School professor who in some ways invented value investing. Graham passed away in 1976, and since the 1990s, the leading value investor has been Warren Buffett, chairman of Berkshire Hathaway, an insurance company with an investment portfolio big enough to make the company resemble a mutual fund in many ways.

Buffett learned his trade at the feet of Graham. Legend has it that Buffett was the only student who ever earned a grade of A+ from Graham.

Over the very long term, Buffett has done well. Some years back, 300 investment managers were asked to name the top money managers of the 20th century. Warren Buffett was number one on more than 86 percent of their lists.

By any measure, beating Buffett represents a very high hurdle. But Buffett has stumbled badly a couple of times. In 1999, a strong bull market propelled the Standard & Poor's 500 Index to gains of 19.5 percent. In that same year, Buffett's portfolio lost 19.9 percent.

Let me repeat to emphasize this point. *In a year that an unmanaged index fund gained 19.5 percent, the man regarded as the best manager of the century lost 19.9 percent.*

After the painful years of 2007 and 2008, the U.S. stock market turned sharply (and quite unexpectedly) upward, gaining more than 25 percent for the year. But Buffett's Berkshire Hathaway rose only 2.7 percent during this raging bull market.

Buffett strays from one cardinal rule of University Street: wide diversification. His portfolio is heavily weighted to insurance and financial companies, some publicly owned and some privately owned. Sometimes, of course, his stock-picking prowess is very successful, and the financial media waste no time in making him a hero. But his relatively concentrated portfolio entails more risks.

If I had to make a bet on a value manager who is likely to beat Buffett in the future, I'd put my money on someone who owned a portfolio of low-cost value funds that included global exposure to large-cap, mid-cap, and small-cap stocks.

I know that the past does not indicate the future. But in the 10 calendar years from 2001 through 2010, a portfolio of five passively managed value funds averaged annual returns of 11.8 percent, more than twice the 5.4 percent return of Berkshire Hathaway stock.

If you can build and keep such a portfolio, then I think *you* have a very good shot at beating Buffett over the long term.

9

THE WORST

"If you find yourself in a hole, stop digging."
—Will Rogers

There are lots of ways investors get in trouble, and I certainly can't warn you about all of them. But I want to alert you to a few potholes and sinkholes that lie on the road toward success. If you can recognize some characteristics of bad investments, perhaps somewhere inside your head warning bells will go off when you come upon something you should avoid.

Here are some of those warning signs:

- Everybody's doing it.
- You can't get your money back for a long time.
- A salesperson is very eager for you to do this.
- The salesperson tells you he or she has just put his or her mother's money into it.
- It seems obviously too good to be true.
- You heard about it in an unsolicited sales call.
- You are told that this investment has outperformed the market for many years.
- The product and its cost structure are hard to understand.
- It seems as if there is no risk involved.
- A majority of the appeal is an expected tax break.
- The strategy is built on borrowed money.
- It's listed on the Securities and Exchange Commission cyberfraud website (http://www.sec.gov/investor/pubs/cyberfraud.htm).

The worst investments fall into four broad categories. There is no reason you should have any of these things in your portfolio.

- The **first category** includes popular investments that are often recommended and generally accepted by commissioned salespeople and retail investors in spite of their drawbacks, including high operating expenses, high turnover, unfavorable tax treatment, and investment fads.

  In the late 1990s when the Internet's dot-com boom was raging, mutual fund companies rushed to put together technology funds. Many of these hit the market just in time to help eager investors lose their shirts. But where were these mutual fund companies when technology stocks were bargains? Doing something else, obviously. Popular, misguided investments aren't insidious frauds. But they are so common that they cost investors more money than all the con artists on earth.

- The **second category** has investments that most professionals know are substandard at best, but they are heavily promoted because they offer very high financial rewards to the sellers. In this chapter you'll meet some examples.

- In the **third category** are Ponzi schemes and other con games that simply have no redeeming value. In a Ponzi scheme, money coming in from new investors is the source of the payout to previous investors. Sooner or later, the scheme collapses. Unfortunately, these phony schemes are not always easy to recognize, and this is one of the reasons that you should always be a bit skeptical.

- The **fourth category** features speculative investments that can cost investors much more than they realize at the start. Let's start by looking at one of those.

The Worst Investment I Ever Made

In 1963, I was a 19-year-old married college student with barely enough money to pay the bills. But I was fascinated with investing and the potential to make money. I read something positive about commodity futures. Then a friendly Merrill Lynch broker encouraged me to invest in a futures contract. To my young mind, it seemed that the universe was lining up to tell me I should do this. I figured I had found a way to make big money in a hurry. So I invested $1,000.

I did get results in a hurry. Within a few weeks I doubled my money. My broker assured me he had another idea that was just as good as the last one, and I immediately reinvested all my money in soybean futures.

I'm sure that broker told me how futures contracts work, but all I remember is being confident that I would soon double my money again. So it's not hard to understand that I was stunned when I was wiped out within a few days.

The experts told me my loss was not the result of bad judgment on my part. They blamed it on an unusually harsh winter in the Midwest. But I was determined to learn everything I could from this experience, and I even made a point to eat a can of soybeans to remind myself of it—a move that quite literally left a bad taste in my mouth that was almost as bad as the loss. I do not recommend eating soybeans, by the way.

It seemed at the time that I had lost $1,000. But now I realize that in fact I lost much more than that. Economists use the phrase "opportunity cost" to describe this. I lost the opportunity to invest that $1,000 sensibly in a low-cost mutual fund that might have grown at approximately market rates. That could easily be worth $100,000 today.

I have to admit that over the years I have invested in some venture capital deals that did not work out as well as if I had put the same money into a well-diversified portfolio. However, I didn't do this with "precious" money that I would someday need to take care of my family.

I knew going in that the risks were high, and I was prepared to lose the money I was investing. I don't encourage people to invest that way unless they are sure that they can lose the whole thing without jeopardizing their present or future lifestyles.

The Worst Mutual Fund Family

There are some excellent mutual fund families, but this chapter is about dogs, so we'll look at the other end of the spectrum. My nomination for this dubious honor is the Oppenheimer family of funds.

There is something very strange to me about the success of Oppenheimer. They manage $152 billion and according to Morningstar, 83 percent of that is in load funds. This means a huge amount of money went into those funds from investors who found Oppenheimer through planners and brokers. I'm puzzled about why these professionals would identify Oppenheimer funds, which rate very low by almost any standard you can measure, as the best solutions for investors.

Expense ratios of Oppenheimer funds are as much as 50 percent higher than those of comparable load funds. The loads on Oppenheimer bond funds are generally a full percentage point higher than those charged by peer funds. Oppenheimer stock funds have above-average portfolio turnover, which drives up shareholders' taxes and costs.

To illustrate how this can play out, and I'll admit this is an extreme example, I want to look at Oppenheimer's Champion Income Fund, a high-yield bond fund that charges front-end loads up to 4.75 percent and expenses of 1.25 percent. The fund's annual portfolio turnover is 144 percent.

In the 10 years that ended May 30, 2011, this fund had a compound return of minus 7.7 percent (a loss). That's for an entire decade. In the three-year period ending the same date, the compound annual loss was an astonishing 32.2 percent. That means investors who bought the fund at the start of June 2008 and held for three years lost nearly 70 percent of their money.

If those investors had been given a choice, they might have put their money instead in another huge load fund family, American Funds. American manages a comparable fund, the American High-Income Trust. Investors pay loads up to 3.75 percent to get into this fund, which has expenses of 0.68 percent (compared with Oppenheimer's 1.25 percent) and an annual portfolio turnover of only 47 percent (Oppenheimer's is 144 percent).

In the 10-year period I mentioned above, American High-Income Trust's annual compound return was positive, 7.9 percent. And in the three years that Oppenheimer shareholders were losing nearly 70 percent of their money, shareholders in American High-Income Trust gained 8.7 percent compounded per year.

Let me put this into real-dollar terms, including the effect of the sales commission. After three years, a $10,000 investment grows to $12,362 if invested in the American High-Income Trust but falls in value to only $2,969 if invested in the Oppenheimer fund.

So why would anybody pay a higher commission in order to invest in the Oppenheimer fund instead of the fund at American Funds? I think the answer has to involve incentives that Oppenheimer pays to attract new money.

Oppenheimer does not have its own sales force. All its sales come through independent commissioned salespeople like brokers and planners. Somehow Oppenheimer has persuaded those people to recommend the company's funds in spite of their high expenses, high portfolio turnover, high sales commissions, and low returns.

If the brokers and planners were working for investors, then those investors should be able to count on the planners and brokers for honest-to-goodness help. But it's Oppenheimer, not investors, that pays the planners, brokers, and brokerage houses. Those professionals know that when they sell the Oppenheimer fund they will make more money. And that's why they sell Oppenheimer instead of American.

This is one of the main reasons I don't trust commissioned salespeople. If they will do this to their clients, what else will they do? Fortunately, lots of investors and salespeople seem to have figured this out. The Oppenheimer fund I just used as an example has total assets of $658 million, according to Morningstar. The one from American Funds is $17.9 billion in size, more than 27 times as large.

The Worst Ways of Wall Street

Three recent films demonstrate the worst practices of Wall Street, and I recommend you devote a few evenings to watching them. They will show you, better than I can tell you, why I believe that the institutions we know collectively as Wall Street are not our friends.

- *Enron: The Smartest Guys in the Room,* a 2005 documentary based on the book of the same title by two reporters for *Fortune*, Bethany McLean and Peter Elkind. The film studies the collapse of Enron, once one of the most admired companies in the United States. The film, nominated for an Academy Award in 2006, shows how little these corporate executives cared about anybody except themselves. If you tend to view big business through rose-colored glasses, this film may change that.

- *Inside Job*, a 2010 documentary about the 2007–2010 financial crisis, won a 2011 Academy Award for Best Documentary Feature. The movie focuses on what Director Charles H. Ferguson called "the systemic corruption of the United States by the financial services industry."

- *Too Big to Fail,* an HBO film by Curtis Lee Hanson that came out in May 2011, is based on a 2009 book of the same name by Andrew Ross Sorkin. An all-star cast, including William Hurt, Cynthia Nixon, James Woods, and Paul Giamatti, focuses on the 2007–2010 financial crisis.

The Worst Investment Scams Aimed at Seniors

I want to emphasize right away that this is only a partial list to give you some examples. Investment scams are like computer viruses. New ones are constantly being invented, and just because something isn't in this discussion doesn't make it a good investment. Investigate before you invest!

Unscrupulous investment promoters have found clever ways to exploit the increasing number of seniors who are worried about low interest rates, estate taxes and probate costs, future inflation, and the supposedly looming threat that our economic system, our government, and our very way of life could soon collapse.

I don't mean to make light of the serious issues facing our society and our economy, but I have no use for people who unscrupulously gain the trust of older people and then use that trust to sell them goods and services they don't need and which can in fact worsen the very problems from which consumers are trying to protect themselves.

Ralph A. Lambiase, director of the Connecticut Division of Securities and president of the North American Securities Administrators Association, deals with these issues daily. "Our fight against fraud never stops because each year con artists discover new ways to fleece the public," he says.

Unfortunately, many financial predators have learned that, with only a slight bit of window dressing, many age-old scams are still very effective at cheating people out of their money.

Variable Annuities

I am reluctant to identify variable annuities as one of the worst investments because they can be valuable in some cases. But I believe that 80 to 90 percent of the people who buy these products eventually wish they had done something else with their money.

Lambiase notes that as more and more variable annuities are sold, more and more people are complaining to him and other regulators. The biggest complaints involve expensive surrender charges and steep sales commissions. Variable annuities are often touted at seminars aimed at seniors, yet Lambiase says they make sense only for people who can afford to lock up their money for 10 years or more.

Essentially, a variable annuity is a collection of proprietary investment pools called subaccounts wrapped inside an insurance policy. The subaccounts have high expenses and offer limited choices of asset classes. The insurance is also expensive, and investors who don't need that insurance have to pay for it anyway.

Variable annuities are often pitched as a great way to save taxes. But they aren't, and few variable annuity investors discover this until it's too late. It's true that earnings inside a variable annuity build up without any current tax liability. That is where the good news stops. In a taxable account, your capital gains and dividends are likely taxed at favorable rates, currently only 15 percent. But when you take those gains and dividends out of your annuity, they are taxed as ordinary income at your highest rate. And that tax is applied to every penny you take out until there is nothing left but your original dollars inside the account. Only then can you get your own money back tax free (because you already paid taxes on it before you invested).

My advice is to avoid variable annuities. In most cases, you can make your money work harder for you elsewhere. If you think you are the exception, then get the advice of a certified public account (C.P.A.) or an independent investment advisor who does not sell insurance products. If such an advisor tells you that your best solution is a variable annuity, then pay that person to walk you through the entire contract, before you sign, and explain in plain English what you are about to agree to.

Equity-Indexed Annuities

A variation of the variable annuity that is popular with salespeople is the equity-indexed annuity. These seem to promise the best of both worlds: a guaranteed minimum interest rate tied to stock market gains when times are good and protection against losses when times are bad.

I have looked at the investment choices offered in the 100 largest 401(k) and similar retirement plans in the United States. Not a single plan offers equity-indexed annuities. Not even one. If this were a good choice for investors, I don't think that would be true.

Alas, there is no free lunch from Wall Street—and certainly not from insurance companies. Equity-indexed annuity contracts are so complex that even some financial planners have had lots of trouble trying to figure out what the insurance company is promising. There are many ways that stock market gains can be defined and limited so that the policies pay out much less than you are led to believe.

Some contracts spell out the details and then give the insurance company the right to change those details later. I can assure you that you'll never be given an insurance company contract that lets *you* change the terms to your benefit. Despite the marketing hype, it's entirely possible to lose money in these products.

The Worst Reason to Choose an Advisor

One day early in 2011, I had a conversation with a woman who admitted she didn't and still doesn't understand investing. But she assured me that she knew "the difference between a good broker and a bad one." The woman told me her daughter had pressured her into meeting with the daughter's broker. The mother immediately disliked the broker, describing him as haughty and inept at explaining things. However, the daughter put the pressure on, and because she didn't want to disappoint her daughter, the woman opened an account.

She told the broker she wanted a low-risk portfolio, and the broker said that was no problem. The daughter had told the broker that her mother needed high returns. Not wanting to disappoint the daughter, the broker focused on high returns. He invested the mother's account in some risky individual stocks, hoping they would skyrocket. They didn't, and the mother lost about half her money in short order. As if that financial fallout wasn't bad enough, this chain of events put a serious strain on the relationship between mother and daughter.

Now, the mother told me, she has a broker she likes much better. The new one fits perfectly into her definition of "a good broker." I asked her why, and she gave me a startled look before saying, "Why, because he's making money for me!"

The backdrop of the story is that the "bad" broker took over the woman's account at the start of a bear market, when almost everything was about to lose money. The "good" one got the account in the early stages of a very robust bull market in which it was easy to make money.

When I was a greenhorn broker in training back in the 1960s, I was told: "You've got to make lots of money during bull markets because nobody wants to buy anything after a big decline." I was taught to expect lots of hard work during bull markets (when customers could easily make money without my advice) and to expect that I would have very little to do during bear markets, ironically when investors could benefit the most from good advice.

From a broker's point of view, the difference between being a hero and a bum may be a matter of lucky—or unlucky—timing. As Will Rogers used to say, "I only buy stocks that go up. If they don't go up, I don't buy 'em."

The Worst Mistake You Can Make as an Investor

When it comes to this topic, it's difficult to narrow the search to just one thing. So I'll take the easy way out and give you five answers from which to choose. Any one of these is potentially lethal. Put them all together, and there's little hope.

- **Trusting advice from others without understanding the investment process.** If you don't take the time to gain an appreciation of things like expenses, taxes, portfolio turnover, asset classes, and risk management, you become the perfect target for people selling products like Oppenheimer load funds. Although you may like the person who gives you the advice, you may never realize that that very advice may be part of the reason you are working longer, sleeping less, worrying more, retiring later, and living on less than you had planned.

- **Trying to beat the market.** I've devoted a whole chapter to this topic because it is such an awful trap. Trying to beat the market can lead you to take too much risk, running up your taxes, your expenses, and your blood pressure. It can become addictive.

  Here's a true story about a Boeing engineer named Doris, obviously a very smart woman, who was among the founders of an investment club and who loved to spend her evenings and weekends on her computer planning stock trades for the next day the market was open. Doris fit right into the era of day-trading.

  Doris had an ample nest egg and was looking forward to retiring in two or three years with a nice pension. She once bragged that she was making profits of 70 percent a month in her individual retirement account (IRA)—a month! (This is Main Street.) And then for some reason that she could never quite explain, Doris's amazing insights and great skill ran smack into a wall.

  In less than a year, Doris lost 70 percent of her portfolio. About the same time, she developed a medical problem that forced her to retire sooner than she and her husband had planned. Suddenly, they were facing a retirement much more bleak than they had envisioned. Instead of living out their retirement dreams and traveling the world, they now live in a modest house in a rural area and stick to a strict budget.

- **Believing that investing is too complicated and difficult to understand.** When I teach high school students the basics, they have no trouble at all understanding them in 45 minutes. This "worst thing you can do" is likely to lead you straight to the first item on this short list—trusting the wrong advisor or mentor.

- **Taking too much risk and then ditching your long-term plans when a bear market turns confidence into panic.** Once you lose your discipline, you will have an awful time getting back in. I believe you are more likely to be successful in the long run if you take less risk and accept less return than if you take more risk in search of higher returns.

- **Waiting to get started.** Young investors often say, "As soon as I get enough money saved, I'm going to get serious about investing." It's understandable, but by waiting they are squandering the most precious resource they will ever have: time. If you invest $1,000 when you're 20 and get a compound return of 10 percent, it will be worth about $72,900 when you're 65. If you wait until you're 30 and get the same 10 percent compound return, your $1,000 investment will be worth only about $28,100 when you're 65. Wait until you're 40, and that $1,000 will grow to be worth only about $10,800 at age 65.

You may not be able to avoid the final mistake on this list. But it's never too late to start doing the right things. A good way to start is by making sure you're not making the big mistakes.

10

TWELVE NUMBERS
TO CHANGE YOUR LIFE

"The beginning is the most important part of the work."
—*Plato*

By this point you may understand what you can and should do to improve your financial future. But understanding, if it's not followed by action, can be the booby prize. You deserve better than that.

What I care about most is changing people's lives. And in this chapter, I'll show you how that happens. Until now this book has dealt in generalities without looking at exactly how they might affect you. Here, your circumstances and your financial fitness become the focus.

If I could have a personal conversation with you, I would cover the topics you will find here. We would go over the most important numbers that every investor who's preparing for retirement should know. If you're already retired, some of these won't apply to you, and that will be obvious. But you may still find this discussion helpful.

If you do your homework and nail down these numbers, you will get a good general picture of your financial fitness. You'll know whether or not you are on track to retire when you want to. If you need to make changes, you'll have the background to figure out what they are.

Over the years I have worked with thousands of people. When they uncover these fundamental facts in an organized way, their circumstances can suddenly become much clearer and less mysterious. I think the same will happen to you.

Finding Your 12 Numbers

The following exercise is one of discovery. There are no right answers or wrong answers. The best answers are the accurate ones. Some are easy;

others are more difficult. I recommend you do your best the first time through and then revisit this topic from time to time as you get closer to retirement.

Let's begin.

Number 1: Your Current Cost of Living

This is the bedrock on which the rest of these exercises are built, so you should later seek an answer that's as accurate as possible. But for now, you can start with a quick-and-dirty approach. Identify your current gross income and then subtract whatever you are saving for the future. (If you have credit card debts that you can't pay off every month, you may be overspending your income, but for this chapter I'll assume that's not the case.)

To show you how these 12 numbers come together, here's a hypothetical example. Start by assuming your two-income household takes in $146,000 a year in gross salaries and that together you and your spouse are aggressive savers, adding $24,000 a year to your retirement nest egg. In this quick-and-dirty calculation, that means your cost of living is about $122,000 a year. This figure includes the income taxes you pay plus Medicare and Social Security payroll taxes.

If you need to get more control over the spending part of your life, or if you want more detail about where your money is going, you can set up an account online at Mint.com (https://www.mint.com/) and let it have access to your bank and credit card accounts. The site will then do its best to categorize your spending into categories that you can track over time.

Monitoring your spending doesn't sound like an investment topic, but in fact it is an essential step while you are planning for retirement. If spending is an issue, this is a very worthwhile place to focus your attention.

Number 2: The Rate of Inflation You Assume for the Future

This is a wild card, but whatever number you choose will have a big effect on your financial future. When I talk to investors, I am most comfortable assuming inflation will be 3.5 percent. That may not seem like much. But over the years it can do more damage than you might think.

Number 3: Number of Years Before You Plan to Retire

This isn't always a simple calculation. You may not be in control of when you retire, for health or other reasons. You may have no intention of ever retiring, just cutting back to part-time work. Or you may want to ease into retirement gradually by reducing your hours in one or more steps before you leave the workforce entirely.

However, in order to keep things relatively simple in this example, I'll assume you are both 55 and you both plan to retire "cold turkey" in 12 years.

Number 4: Your Inflation-Adjusted Cost of Living After You Retire

This can be a complicated number to pin down because you have to try to anticipate things that will change. Some of them won't be under your control, some will. Some changes will be major, others will have less impact on your finances.

Some people plan to move closer to their kids. Others plan to move to a better climate or to an area with lower housing prices. (If this describes you, don't forget the one-time cost of the move itself.)

After you retire you may find yourself with much more time to pursue hobbies and travel. You may find that you are spending more money than you are accustomed to. You'll probably pay less for commuting and clothes, and you won't need to keep contributing to your retirement plans.

Your taxes will change, too. After you retire you won't have to pay Social Security and Medicare taxes. I'm going to assume that the bulk of your retirement savings are in rollover individual retirement accounts (IRAs) and 401(k) plans. That means that withdrawals from them will be fully taxable. I also assume that your Social Security and pension will be taxable as well.

For our example, I'll fill in the blanks with some more made-up numbers in order to show how this series of calculations works.

To your current $122,000 cost of living, I'm adding $5,000 to cover what I assume will be higher health care costs plus another $3,000 for travel in addition to whatever you are spending now. The latter is an optional expense that you can reduce if necessary, and that makes it a bit of a cushion. That brings your total to $130,000.

On the other hand, I estimate you can subtract $6,000 that you will no longer have to pay for commuting and various other business costs. I'm also subtracting $10,000 in Social Security and Medicare taxes. You have nine years to go on your mortgage, which will be paid off three years before you retire. That will save you about $32,000 a year in retirement. In addition, as I complete another step in this process I will assume you will add that $32,000 to your retirement savings for the last three years.

The net of all these changes projects $82,000 as the cost of living during your first year of retirement.

That number is stated in current dollars, before adjusting for inflation. If you have access to a financial calculator or know your way around a computer spreadsheet, it's easy to adjust this for 12 years of 3.5 percent inflation. The result is an inflation-adjusted cost of living that's about $124,000. (Remember, these are future dollars, and that's why the number seems so big.)

Item	Your Number
Present cost of living	$122,000
Assumed future inflation	3.5%
Years until retirement	12 years
Cost of living 1st year of retirement	$124,000

By necessity, this number is built on many assumptions, guesses, and estimates. Accordingly, I don't totally trust it. But you have 12 years to refine this, and for now that number is good enough to give you an idea of where you stand. Therefore, we'll assume you will need $124,000 in your first year of retirement.

Now we want to know where that $124,000 will come from.

Number 5: Retirement Income You Can Count On

For most people, this category will include Social Security. It might also include a pension, rental income, or notes receivable. For this calculation, don't include investment income such as interest, dividends, or expected capital gains.

I'll assume that you and your spouse will collect $36,000 in Social Security and that you will have a pension of $13,000 a year from a previous job. If we assume that these figures don't have to be adjusted for future inflation and we add them together, you will have $49,000 you can count on.

Number 6: Retirement Income You'll Need Every Year from Your Portfolio

This requires nothing more than elementary-school math. You need $124,000 when you retire. You can count on $49,000, which leaves $75,000 that must come from somewhere else.

Number 7: Portfolio You'll Need at Retirement

If your investments are properly balanced between well-diversified stock funds and bond funds, you can get a quick-and-dirty answer in this step by multiplying $75,000 by 25. This assumes you will withdraw 4 percent of your portfolio's value the first year you're retired and then adjust the number every subsequent year to cover inflation.

(Please note that a withdrawal rate of 4 percent may or may not be appropriate for you. Your circumstances may dictate something different. I highly recommend studying Appendix H, "Withdrawing Money when You're Retired," which goes into this topic in detail.)

Four percent is a conservative withdrawal rate that will minimize your risk of running out of money. To support that, you have to have a big portfolio. In your case, that means you will need $1,875,000 worth of investments when you retire.

This is not an exact number by any means. We tossed precision out the window when we put together all our assumptions and estimates and then multiplied the result by 25.

The $1,875,000 target is the bad news. The good news is that you still have 12 years before you retire. That's plenty of time in which to refine your objectives, find ways to invest better, and save more.

Number 8: The Current Size of Your Investment Portfolio

This number should include only your investments, excluding real estate and other nonliquid assets. In addition to stocks, bonds, mutual funds, IRAs, 401(k)s, and similar accounts, your portfolio may include cash, certificates of deposit, Treasury bills, or notes as well as loans

Item	Your Number
Present cost of living	$122,000
Assumed future inflation	3.5%
Years until retirement	12 years
Cost of living 1st year of retirement	$124,000
Fixed retirement income	$49,000
Income needed from investments	$75,000
Portfolio size at retirement	$1,875,000

payable to you that you reasonably expect to be paid by the time you retire.

To continue our calculations, I'm going to assume you have been aggressive savers and your portfolio is worth $510,000 right now. In the next few steps, we'll find out what's necessary for it to grow to $1,875,000 in 12 years.

Number 9: Your Annual Retirement Savings

Actually, we already know this number from our very first calculation. You and your spouse are saving $24,000 a year. If you keep that up, you will add $288,000 to your portfolio over the 12 years plus $96,000 in the last 3 years when your mortgage is paid off. If your investments didn't make any money or lose any money in the meantime, you would have $894,000, leaving you far short of your target. That's why you need growth in your portfolio.

Number 10: The Annual Return You Need from Now Until You Retire

To figure this out, you'll need a financial calculator or a computer spreadsheet.

Based on the numbers that we just outlined and your goal of having $1,875,000 in 12 years, my calculator tells me that you can get there if your money grows at an annualized rate of 8.1 percent. That's in the ballpark of historical returns for well-diversified portfolios with very moderate levels of risk.

It has taken a lot of work to get to that number. But now we can see that you have a shot at meeting your goal if you invest prudently and keep your expenses under control.

Nobody can tell you what investment returns will be over the next 12 years, so there is no guarantee of anything. You'll find a table of long-term returns in Appendix B, "Fine-Tuning Your Asset Allocation," which looks at levels of risk and return going back to 1970 for portfolios with various combinations of stocks and bonds. Though this table is only a very approximate guide to the future, I think it is encouraging in your situation.

From 1970 through 2010, a relatively low-risk portfolio with 60 percent in properly diversified stock funds and 40 percent in bond funds achieved an annualized return of 10.6 percent—definitely higher than the 8.1 percent you need.

Even if we assume that over the next 12 years such a portfolio would achieve two full percentage points less than that, or 8.6 percent, that would still be above what you need.

Having 60 percent of your portfolio in stock funds unquestionably subjects you to some risk, and you should carefully consider this. In the 41 years we just examined, that 60 percent equity portfolio's worst 12-month loss was 33.5 percent. That would be a significant setback for you, and if it occurred just before or just after you retired, you would have to modify your expectations.

Because in this chapter "you" are purely a hypothetical creature who exists only in my imagination, I'm in charge of you. Therefore, I can say on good authority that you and your spouse are sensible enough and resilient enough that you would be willing and able to work longer or scale back your retirement spending plans—or perhaps both—until you recovered.

I started this chapter with the promise of 12 numbers that can change your financial future. Two more remain that will help you improve your financial fitness and have the future you want.

Number 11: The Overall Stock Allocation of Your Portfolio Now

If you have most or all of your investments in one place, you may already know this figure. But many investors have to dig a bit to figure this one out. A financial software program such as Quicken can help, if you use it to keep track of your holdings. If your portfolio consists of stocks, exchange-traded funds (ETFs), and mutual funds, you can use the Portfolio X-Ray tool at Morningstar (http://www.morningstar .com/) to determine your overall exposure to stocks and bonds.

For purposes of this example, I'm going to assume we have discovered that your current allocation is 84 percent stocks and 16 percent bonds. I think that is too aggressive for somebody within 12 years of retirement, and I think it means that you are subjecting yourself and your family to more risk than is necessary. Fortunately, we can make a pretty good estimate of this.

Number 12: The Amount of Risk in Your Portfolio Now

If you have 84 percent of your portfolio in stock funds, the full version of the table in Appendix B, "Fine-Tuning Your Asset Allocation," leads me to conclude that you're exposed to the risk of losing 45 percent of your portfolio in some 12-month period. This assumes your stock holdings are well diversified. If that's not the case, your risk exposure is probably higher.

Even exceptionally good investors and sensible people like you and your spouse would have a hard time recovering from a loss of 45 percent or more. Fortunately, you don't need to take that much risk.

Item	Your Number
Present cost of living	$122,000
Assumed future inflation	3.5%
Years until retirement	12 years
Cost of living 1st year of retirement	$124,000
Fixed retirement income	$49,000
Income needed from investments	$75,000
Portfolio size at retirement	$1,875,000
Portfolio size now	$510,000
Annual savings	$24,000
Investment return needed	8.1%
Current allocation to stocks	84%
Current risk exposure (12-month loss)	45%

Where Do You Go from Here?

Now we are ready to discuss what you can do to maximize your chances of meeting your retirement goals. If I were meeting with you and your spouse, based on what I know of your circumstances I would probably tell you the most important thing you can do is reduce the amount of risk you are taking.

Over the last four decades, if you had invested 40 percent of your money in a well-diversified group of stock funds and the other 60 percent in bond funds, your greatest 12-month loss would have been 23.1 percent. A 40 percent equity portfolio represents a much more conservative approach than you are now taking. And the good news is that, over that same period, your annualized return in such a portfolio would have been 9.4 percent—higher than you need.

However, I don't know how likely it is that this conservative allocation will earn that level of return over the next 12 years, and I think a higher equity allocation is more likely to be successful for you.

Your Action Plan

The last step in this process is to think about what changes you need or want to make. You have achieved a good platform on which to build the rest of your nest egg. Now you need to keep building and defend your position at the same time.

Faced with the facts in this hypothetical scenario, I have three recommendations.

1. Rebalance your portfolio in order to scale your stock exposure to no more than 60 percent; in your case, 50 percent might be sufficient to meet your goals, and I prefer that slightly more conservative allocation. But since you and your spouse are good savers as well as reasonable and resilient, I would not try to talk you out of a 60 percent equity portfolio if you want a slightly higher expected return.

2. Have a conversation in which you go over these numbers and projections with your spouse. Include your grown children if that is appropriate. Do your best to obtain their support for continuing your savings and keeping your expenses under control.

3. Keep your calculations, either on paper or in a computer file, where you can find them easily. Every year, update the numbers to keep abreast of your changing portfolio value, your living expenses, and inflation. The changes may be very minor in any one year, but things will change, and you should keep fine-tuning your calculations to make sure you're still on track. Once you've done this a few times, it will become easy and you'll recognize the records you should be keeping for this exercise.

Perhaps the Best Investment You Can Make

I do live in the real world, and I know that most people won't do all these things, even though we've seen how valuable this exercise can be. Rounding up the numbers can be daunting, and there are multiple places where you may feel like throwing up your hands because of information you simply don't have—or information that you don't want to face up to.

However, I believe this exercise is absolutely necessary if you want to maximize your financial fitness in preparation for retiring.

Here's my final recommendation. Get a professional to help you with these things:

- If you are using a financial advisor or you're thinking of hiring one, he or she should be able to help you with all these numbers and then figure out the appropriate action plan. This is a huge benefit of having an advisor.

- If you aren't interested in taking that route, find somebody to help you with this on an hourly basis. A certified public accountant (C.P.A.) with training in personal finance could certainly help you arrive at the numbers you need. I know that C.P.A.s often have time available after their busy tax season, January through April. A certified financial planner can also do this for you. If all you want is expert help with the exercises in this chapter, make sure you choose somebody who's willing to work for an hourly fee and who does not sell financial products.

For more on choosing a good advisor, see Appendix I, "Hiring an Investment Advisor."

If you do your homework well and do a good job of calculating these 12 numbers, I'm very confident that it will be well worth your efforts.

I can't guarantee that you'll like the results of such a "financial fitness checkup." But when you're done, you will have the facts. Once you know the facts, you can figure out a plan to achieve the retirement you want.

In the second paragraph of this chapter, I told you that what I care about most is changing people's lives. Now you have seen exactly how that happens.

11

THE PERFECT
INVESTOR

*"We are what we repeatedly do. Excellence comes not
from our actions but from our habits."*
—Aristotle

This chapter has its origins in an around-the-table discussion at our company in the summer of 2010. Several of us, including my son, Jeff Merriman-Cohen, and my writing partner, Richard Buck, were brainstorming possible topics for a new project that we thought might possibly become a book.

We considered describing the theoretically perfect investment. This could contain a lot of useful information that investors need to know. However, we quickly realized we had already done that elsewhere.

We thought about describing the perfect investment advisor. While this is an extremely important topic, it didn't seem quite right for a whole book aimed at general audiences.

Then a new idea popped up. What about describing the perfect investor? We couldn't find any book with a title like that, and it seemed like a good possibility. We are certainly qualified to write on that topic, based on nearly 30 years of working with thousands of clients. The more we talked, the more intrigued we became.

A few investors are lucky enough to be successful primarily because they were born into wealth and abundance. But the vast majority of us have to rely on hard work and . . . what else?

Naturally, we were pretty sure that we could identify the traits of the perfect investor. But we wanted to create something more than a lecture. We wanted something that was totally authentic and deeply rooted in the experiences and stories of real-life investors.

Over the next several weeks, we held a series of meetings with our financial advisors to tap into their experiences. What is that elusive "what else"? Who were the most successful investors our advisors have known, regardless of how much money they had? What sets those investors apart from others? We purposely left the definition of *successful* a bit vague because we believed that nobody could recognize success (or the lack of it) better than investment advisors—professionals who spend their working lives "in the trenches" with investors.

Almost immediately, we identified some common themes. As the "secrets of success" began to emerge, we could see that there really wasn't anything secret or mysterious about them.

In fact, much of what we were hearing sounded like a description of attitudes and habits that contribute to success in life in general. This didn't surprise us, though we think it's an important point to note.

In a nutshell, here's the core of what we learned: the "perfect investor," if such a person really exists, is somebody who plans for the future and is patient and deliberate in carrying out those plans. In this case, I think perfection could be distilled into three *P* words: *patience, planning*, and *persistence*.

The practice of perfection comes down to two things: our attitudes and our habits.

Attitudes

Our attitudes shape our behavior almost automatically when we aren't watching. As such, they exert a very powerful influence on the quality of our lives. To some extent our attitudes are built into our individual makeup and can be tough to change. But in the end, you are the only one who is in control of your attitudes. No matter what the circumstances, you bring a point of view to the table. That point of view makes a big difference.

We identified five key attitudes of the most successful investors.

Trust can be tricky. If you trust too easily, or trust the wrong idea or person, you can get yourself in trouble fast. But on the other hand, if you're unwilling to trust anything or anybody, you can't build a good future.

We've recently lived through times when companies, individuals, and institutions that seemed rock-solid appeared to crumble before our eyes. Some investors found it nearly impossible to trust anything or anybody. However, trust is a necessary component of success.

When you invest money, you must take a leap of faith. When you take that leap, you have to be confident that you'll have somewhere safe to land. Successful investors, we have observed, seem to have faith in the future despite the problems of today.

I can't prove there's a future in which you will be rewarded for doing the right things. But I am quite sure that your future will be better if you do the right things than if you don't.

Resilience is something every parent sees in children as they learn to crawl, walk, talk, and then (fill in the blank). Time and again, children fall and then try again as often as it takes. Throughout our lives, we stumble, bumble, and demonstrate just how imperfect we are. And we never outgrow our need to be willing to pick ourselves up, dust ourselves off, and try again.

In this book we have seen some of the ways investors make mistakes. On top of that, the markets throw lots of curveballs our way. Every investor runs into rough spots. Some are only bumps in the road, while others are chasms that seem to have no bottom. The most successful investors, like the most successful people, are those who are willing and able to bounce back even from serious adversities.

Winston Churchill achieved great things despite a lifetime of serious setbacks. To the end, he maintained a fierce resilience that was summed up in something he repeated many times, "No matter what, never give up."

Perspective is easy to lose in the excitement of bull markets and bear markets and events that seem like economic or political meltdowns. It's a cliché, but a useful one, that when all you can see are trees, you may not notice that you're in a forest.

The most successful investors can deal competently with little things and big ones. They can tell the difference between what's unimportant and what is important. They can look beyond their short-term concerns to focus on what's most likely to bring them success in the long run.

I can't give you the perspective you need. But I can tell you where I often find it for myself—from professional advisors and trusted friends who know me well. No matter how smart I think I am, no matter how much I think I know, I'm constantly amazed by how easy it can be for somebody else to see what I am not seeing—even when it's right in front of me.

Patience may seem obvious, but as we have seen time and again in the pages of this book, impatience can be a ticket to trouble. Rome, as they say, wasn't built in a day. Neither was any retirement portfolio that I know of. The most successful investors understand that time is their ally, and they can wait for results. The least successful investors are more likely to be upset—or elated as the case may be—by what's happening at any given moment in the market.

If you are following a sound plan to invest money that you won't need for years or decades, what happens to your investments next week or next month is not of huge consequence. Do you remember what was happening in the market exactly five years ago today? Ten years ago today? I didn't think so. I don't either, and by now it really doesn't matter. This leads me to a fifth valuable attitude.

I'm almost afraid to mention *common sense* because this term is used to mean so many things. In fact, the notion of common sense can be used to justify almost anything you may feel like doing. That's the bad side of common sense.

What I recommend is the good side of common sense. Our advisors have noticed that successful investors apply common sense as a reality check before they make important decisions. Here are two examples of what I regard as common sense.

First, if you hear about an investment that offers very attractive returns without any risk, you can be certain that you are missing something. Frequently I hear about sales pitches for products that seem to pay much more than you could get at any bank, yet with little or no risk.

Common sense will lead you in the right direction if you ask yourself one simple question. If an investment is really as wonderful as it is made out to be, why hasn't it been snapped up by the full-time money managers who are always looking for good places to invest the money at their disposal?

Information moves so easily and quickly, and greed is so rampant, that I can virtually guarantee that many millions (if not billions) of dollars would instantly flow into any risk-free investment paying significantly more than bank account rates. If such an opportunity is being offered to you, common sense will tell you that, for whatever reason, the "big money" doesn't want that opportunity. And if the professionals don't want it, should you?

If you believe the aggressive pitches of commissioned salespeople, equity-indexed annuities are practically the best investment ever invented. Yet I don't know of a single pension fund that has any of these products in its portfolio. Common sense should lead you to wonder why that is the case.

My second example of common sense is about saving. If you're counting on having a comfortable retirement, the money for it is not likely to fall into your lap. If you don't save dollars now, you won't have them to spend later. This is about as obvious as you can get, and it's sometimes expressed as "You can spend a dollar only once." It's pure common sense, but you might be surprised to know how many people never seem to figure this out.

Habits

Habits are a lot like attitudes. They govern our behavior in the background and let us move through life without requiring us to think about the same issue again and again.

Because habits are about behavior, they may be easier to change than attitudes. When you drive, you might never make a conscious decision to use your turn signals or stop at yellow lights instead of racing through them. But you can get in the habit of doing those things anyway. And when you change or adopt a habit, your attitude may follow.

Some habits are destructive. But I'm interested in the good ones that can help you be a better investor. Here are six.

1. Successful investors know where they are going and set goals for getting there (see Chapter 10, "Twelve Numbers to Change Your Life"). It's easy, especially when you think you're many years away from retiring, to wander aimlessly among all the investment options available to you. And if you don't have a clearly articulated and measurable goal, you might think wandering is enough. However, once you set some fixed goals, your investment choices and actions acquire an entirely new meaning. Like a casual traveler who has been handed a road map and a destination, you can suddenly know what you should do.

2. Successful investors make plans to achieve their goals, and then follow the plans. Is this really a habit? I think so. In the ivory tower view of life, an investor sets goals once, makes plans once, and merrily carries out those plans forever. But

in the real world, our needs change, circumstances change, knowledge evolves. Thinking about your goals and working to achieve them can become a regular part of your life. I recommend it.

3. Successful investors save regularly and routinely. In our roundtable discussions among advisors, this was the very first trait that emerged. Every advisor we talked to agreed that this is an absolutely essential ingredient for successful long-term investing. After all, you can't invest money unless you have it, and unless you save it, you probably won't have it.

    The best investors find ways to add to their savings automatically. These days, that is pretty easy to do through payroll deductions and regularly scheduled online transfers. If you want to be like the best investors we know, this is one easy way to do it.

4. Successful investors make a practice of delaying gratification and living below their means. This, of course, is an essential habit in order to save money. If you know from experience that you can live on less if necessary, then you've laid an important piece of groundwork for a successful retirement.

    Some of the best investors we know make it a point of pride to demonstrate that they can live on less and still be happy. They're the ones most likely to enjoy retirement, for they have managed to cut the emotional cord between how much money they have and how happy they are.

5. Successful investors have emotions, but they don't let greed blind them, and they don't let fear spook them. This isn't always easy. In 2008 and the first quarter of 2009, the financial news was truly awful, and fear ran rampant. Our financial advisors spent hundreds of hours on the phone with clients who wanted to bail out of the market. Some of those investors did bail out, despite our best efforts to help.

    However, the most successful investors were the ones who could step back from their fear, regain their perspective, find ways to comfort themselves—and continue to follow their plans. Many people reevaluated their risk tolerance and adopted a more conservative stance. But they remained in the game, and that paid off later in 2009 and 2010 as the market recovered.

It works the same way in reverse, too. In the great bull market of 1995 through 1999, stock investors seemed to be able to make money easily, especially in technology stocks. Day-trading became very popular, and some people took out credit card loans and second mortgages to invest in stocks. Some investors found it extremely challenging emotionally to own low-yielding bond funds or follow our advice to diversify into value funds and international funds.

However, the most successful investors back then were those who reined in their greed and kept using thorough diversification and bond funds to protect themselves against risk. That paid off in the severe bear market of 2000 through 2002.

The same thing happened again a few years later, when a very robust recovery in 2003 through 2007 was followed by an awful bear market in late 2007 through early 2009, which in turn was followed by a stunningly unexpected recovery from the spring of 2009 through 2010.

6. Successful investors expect setbacks and stay in the game anyway. I remember opening an account some years back for a woman who had inherited some money from her mother and wanted it to be the start of her retirement fund. When I was dealing directly with clients, I was always very careful to prepare them for tough times, and I did my best to let this woman know she would face some setbacks along the way.

    She seemed fine with that idea. Then almost exactly a month after she opened the account, she called our office and closed it, asking for a check. She had lost about 1 percent of her portfolio in that month.

    I got her on the phone and asked her if she remembered our discussion about the fact that sometimes the market wouldn't be kind to her. Yes, she remembered. I asked if she remembered my promise that she would experience some temporary losses along the way. She remembered. I asked if she remembered her promise to stick with it when that happened. She said she remembered.

"Then why are you closing your account after only a month?" I asked. I've never forgotten her reply: "I thought that we would make some money first before I lost it."

Had this woman remained invested, her portfolio would have gone up nearly 10 percent in the following eight months. But by quitting prematurely, she locked in her loss and gave up a perfectly sensible game plan.

Successful investors stay the course in spite of the setbacks they inevitably encounter. This is resilience in action.

Perfection and You

Can you do all these things? What I've just outlined may seem like a pretty tough assignment, and in a way it is. I'm telling you how to be outstandingly successful, and that means doing what most other people don't do. The good news is that most if not all of these attitudes and habits are within your control.

However, pure perfection exists only in textbooks. We are fallible humans who live in an imperfect world. So my parting advice to you is this: give yourself—and the world—a little slack. I haven't lived my life perfectly, and you won't live yours perfectly.

Sometimes, the things you know, the things you expect, and the things you do may let you down.

However, if you do your best to do your best, and if you determine to keep putting yourself back in the game, you'll be the best investor that you can be. In my book, that's as close to perfect as it gets.

APPENDIX A
Asset Allocation

In this appendix I introduce some of the many asset allocation approaches you can use to determine the best balance of fixed-income and equity investments to meet your needs. This discussion is aimed at arriving at only two numbers—the percentage you'll hold in stock funds and the percentage in fixed-income funds. (They should add up to 100, so, in fact, we might be looking for only one number.) If those numbers are 60 and 40, respectively, then 60 percent of your portfolio is allocated to various stock funds and the other 40 percent to fixed-income funds. I recommend, and for this discussion I assume, that you will diversify your assets properly within each of these two parts of your portfolio.

Here are 10 approaches to finding the right balance.

1. I always like investment decisions that can be made automatically, without letting emotions take over. An often-cited asset allocation formula asks you to subtract your age from 100 and then put that percentage into stock funds, with the rest going to bonds. Stated another way, your current age tells you the percentage you should hold in bonds. This is easy to calculate and very conservative because it uses a hefty dosage of bonds even for young investors. I think it's too conservative. It seeks to protect young investors from falling stock prices (30 percent in bonds for a 30-year-old) even though falling stock prices can be beneficial to people who are putting money aside. And this formula deprives older retirees of some of the equities I think they need in order to keep up with inflation.

2. The previous formula can be improved by subtracting your age from 110 or 120 instead of 100. This will give you an additional 10 to 20 percentage points in equities, and over time I believe that is likely to add 0.5 to 1 percentage point to your return. That may seem insignificant, but over a lifetime it can easily add $500,000 to $1 million to your retirement savings.

3. I believe in defensive investment strategies, but defense is not necessarily the best approach when you are young. Young investors who understand the benefits of bear markets for accumulators should have 100 percent of their retirement investments in a diversified portfolio of equities. However, their portfolios should become less aggressive as they get older. Here's a simple formula for doing that, one I think can work well for many people. When you reach age 35, move 10 percent (if you consider yourself aggressive) or 20 percent (if you feel conservative) of your portfolio into bond funds. Every five years after that, move another 5 percent of your portfolio into bond funds. At age 65, this leaves an aggressive investor with 40 percent in bonds and a conservative investor with 50 percent in bonds. Those are good allocations that many retirees can live with the rest of their lives.

4. Another legitimate asset allocation approach for the rest of your life is to invest in a target-date retirement fund. I discussed these briefly in Chapter 8, "The Best," noting that Vanguard has low-cost entries in this category. This approach is as simple and automatic as it gets. One decision lasts for life. But there's a cost for this simplicity. I believe investors in these funds will give up 1 percent to 2 percent in returns every year. Target-date funds tend to be overweighted in fixed income, and their equity holdings have too little exposure to international stocks, small-company stocks, and value stocks. If you're going to take this route, I strongly advise consulting with a professional to make sure you get what's right for you. Target-date retirement funds assume that the only thing that determines your risk tolerance is the year you plan to retire. If only investing were that simple! When you buy a target-date fund, you are making one decision for life. Before you do that, I hope you will go to whatever trouble and expense is necessary to make sure it's a decision you can live with.

5. You might start by determining how much of your portfolio, in percentage terms, you believe you will be willing to lose without abandoning your long-term strategy, and then find the asset allocation "sweet spot" that would give you the highest return while keeping you within your range of risk tolerance. The table in Appendix B, "Fine-Tuning Your Asset Allocation," gives you a good tool for this, based on more than four decades of investment returns and risks. If you take this approach, I recommend you work with a professional investment advisor to periodically review your portfolio and talk about whether this is still the right long-term strategy for you.

6. Consider the inverse of what I just described. Start by figuring out how much long-term return you need in order ·to reach your goals and then use the table in Appendix B to find the lowest-risk way to seek that return. One danger with this approach is that your desired or needed return may require too much risk for your comfort. This is where the rubber meets the road in asset allocation, and you may have to do some soul-searching to navigate through this territory.

   I have talked to a lot of people who grappled with this situation, and my advice is unequivocal. Don't push yourself beyond your comfort zone in order to try to earn a high return. This will almost certainly lead you to abandon your strategy and wind up with less than if you had pursued a more moderate course. Instead, stay within your comfort zone and reduce your need for return by saving more, working longer, planning to live on less in retirement, or working part-time after you retire—or quite likely some combination of those.

7. Some retired investors who are living off their incomes are spooked at the thought of having any of their money at all exposed to the risk of the stock market. Yet often they realize they need more inflation protection than they can get from fixed-income funds. If that describes you, consider the following approach, which has worked for many investors I know. Put enough of your portfolio into the bond funds that I recommend in Appendix C, "The Ultimate Buy-and-Hold Strategy," so that the interest meets your cash flow needs. The rest of your portfolio goes into stock funds. When inflation pushes your needs above the interest you get from the bond funds,

supplement that income by withdrawing money from the stock funds.

Here's an example. The monthly income portfolio I recommend, as I write this, has a current yield of 4.4 percent. Suppose you have a $1 million portfolio from which you need $35,000 a year. You can obtain that income by putting $800,000 into the four fixed-income funds, leaving $200,000 for stock funds.

8. If you have accumulated enough assets to meet your needs, for heaven's sake scale back your level of risk to become more defensive. You should do this even if you continue to work and add money to your portfolio. I think you should aspire to reach the ultimate in financial luxury, when you can take less risk and sleep soundly. Unfortunately, many people have trouble knowing when enough is truly enough. By 1999, the technology bubble had produced sufficient wealth for many investors to retire without worry, even though they planned to keep on working. Many of them made the mistake of continuing to take unnecessary risks, which led to big (and unnecessary) losses in the bear market of 2000 through 2002. You may never reach the point where you're sure you have it made. But if you do, I hope you will reduce the amount of risk you are taking so you don't have to start over building your wealth.

9. One of the most amazing things I have learned over the years is how easily an investor can turn a relatively conservative portfolio into a bonanza. Some years ago we wrote an article entitled "One Portfolio for Life" that advocated a lifetime allocation of 60 percent equity and 40 percent fixed income. Granted, this is probably too conservative for many investors in their 20s and 30s, and it may be too aggressive for many retirees. But I continue to think that this allocation, while not perfect, will protect investors from the worst ravages of bear markets and will give them the growth they need as they accumulate assets and the inflation protection they need when they are retired.

I studied this allocation back to 1927, and here's what I found. If you owned a portfolio that was 60 percent in diversified equities and 40 percent in five-year government bonds, your return was almost exactly the same as if you had owned only the S&P 500 Index—with only about 40 percent of the risk. To measure this, we studied periods that lasted 120 months, or 10 years, and we used monthly returns. From 1927 through 2010, there were 877 10-year periods. We found that the S&P lost money in 53 of those periods. Let me say it again. There were 53 times when an investor in the U.S. stock market's premier index could look back over 10 years and find a loss. The 60/40 portfolio I just described never had one—*not even one*—losing 10-year period.

Actually, the story is even better for today's investors, who have easy access to more asset classes that have outperformed the S&P 500 while still reducing risk. For example, the 60 percent equity portfolio I just described returned 7.5 percent a year for the 10 years ending December 31, 2010; with the added asset classes I recommend, that portfolio returned 8.9 percent a year. Remember, those numbers cover a period that many people have called "the lost decade." Yes, this decade was lost for many investors. But those who diversified well, did well.

10. Finally, I want to share something a bright young investor told me that kept him from throwing in the towel during the nasty 2007–2009 bear market. This man was 34, had a good job at a big technology company in California, and had very good savings habits. I was startled to learn that he had been keeping 20 percent of his portfolio in the bond funds I had recommended over the years. I told him I couldn't believe that 20 percent in bonds was enough to keep him from losing a lot of money in the bear market. He agreed that it wasn't. But he told me that those bond funds kept him in the game because he knew he couldn't lose everything he had set aside for his future. If you think a similar approach will work for you, I encourage you to give it serious consideration.

I hope that somewhere in this list you will find an asset allocation strategy that fits your own needs. No matter how much or how little you have invested, it's worth your while to find the right allocation formula that will give you both peace of mind and a piece of the action. If you have that, in my book you have it made.

APPENDIX B
Fine-Tuning
Your Asset Allocation

Perhaps the biggest job any investor has is managing risk. If you take too much, you could be flirting with disaster; if you take too little, you could cheat yourself out of the returns you need to take care of yourself, your family, and your heirs. In this appendix, I show you how to get this important equation right.

One of the most fundamental decisions faced by every investor is how to allocate a portfolio between stock funds and bond funds. Some investors prefer an all-equity portfolio for its superior long-term growth prospects. Others invest exclusively in fixed-income instruments, preferring to completely avoid the risks of the stock market. But in my experience most people are more comfortable somewhere in between those two extremes.

Moderation is a great virtue, especially when it is applied to the tradeoff between seeking returns and seeking to minimize risk. Many percentage combinations of equities and bonds are possible. Here, I'll concentrate on just three. I believe that one of them is likely to be a very good choice for most long-term investors.

At the end of this appendix, reprinted with permission from Merriman, Inc., is a table of year-by-year returns from 1970 through 2010 for three allocation combinations: 40 percent equities, 50 percent equities, and 60 percent equities. A fourth column shows the comparable numbers for the Standard & Poor's 500 Index, widely considered a proxy for the U.S. stock market.

While the annual returns are interesting, I believe the most useful part of the table is at the bottom where I show the worst-case periods an investor would have experienced in each of those combinations. I'm focused on the bad times because successful investors must persevere through them if they hope to achieve long-term returns like those shown in the table.

Throughout this book I have emphasized the importance of properly diversifying assets, particularly the equity side of your portfolio. Whether your portfolio has 100 percent in equities or only 10 percent in equities, those equities should include U.S. and international stocks, large-cap and small-cap stocks, and value stocks and growth stocks.

That wide diversification gives investors excellent representation in all the major markets. It's also very easy to understand. No matter what major asset class is performing the best at any given time, such a portfolio will own it. You'll find our detailed recommendations and the reasons for them in Appendix C, "The Ultimate Buy-and-Hold Strategy."

The numbers in this table are based on the mix of assets that we recommend. I've included the Standard & Poor's 500 Index not because I recommend it but for comparison to show the benefit of a more moderate approach.

To see the benefit of proper diversification, look at the "Annualized Return" line in the table. You'll see that the index, representing mostly U.S. large-company stocks, had the same 41-year compound return—10 percent—as the 50 percent equity portfolio. That diversification added so much value that it required only half as much equity exposure to achieve the same return.

The "Standard Deviation" line shows the payoff. Volatility, an objective measure of risk, was only 8.2 percent for the 50 percent equity portfolio, compared with 15.7 percent for the S&P 500 Index. (The key thing about this statistic is that lower numbers mean lower volatility.)

Those numbers, of course, are abstract. But some other comparisons may be easier to grasp immediately. You'll see that the worst month in the 50 percent equity strategy was a loss of 12.8 percent, considerably less awful than the one-month loss of 21.5 percent in the Standard & Poor's 500 Index. Long-term investors in the 50 percent equity strategy endured a loss of 2.7 percent in some 60-month period; but the comparable loss in the S&P 500 Index was 29.1 percent—a performance that is very hard to stomach when it lasts five years. Note that these are not calendar years. For these lines in this table, any "worst" period could start at the beginning of any month.

The annual returns in the 50 percent equity column make another interesting comparison with those of the Standard & Poor's 500 Index. The 50/50 portfolio had five calendar years with losses that averaged 8.5

percent; the index came up short in nine calendar years with an average loss of 15.2 percent.

In Appendix C, "The Ultimate Buy-and-Hold Strategy," I show how to put together a portfolio with 60 percent in equity funds and 40 percent in bond funds. I regard this combination as a very good tradeoff between the long-term returns of the world's stock markets and the lower volatility of bond funds. You can look at the numbers in this table to see how they compare with the others there.

There's a reason that the figures at the bottom of this table are negative, concentrating on losses. Risk and losses are not pleasant topics. But you will be far better off if you spend some time with them instead of concentrating on the fabulous returns you hope to achieve. In real life, you'll never get those returns if you don't stick with the program you select. And you won't stick with the program if normal market fluctuations push you out of your comfort zone and prompt you to sell your holdings after you have sustained significant losses and things look bleak.

The reason we pay so much attention to measuring and managing risks is that this is exactly where so many investors get tripped up.

The Return You Want Versus the Return You Need

Investors often tell me they want the highest possible returns. But when I suggest that they put all their money in pork belly futures contracts or bet their life savings on Google stock, they quickly change their tunes. Still, if you are like most people you want as much as you can get. The critical point here is that you can't get a return unless you are invested in the portfolio that produces it. If you are scared off the playing field and onto the sidelines because of inappropriately high risks, you won't be in the game.

But what if you need the returns from a combination that has more risk than you want to take? Your first impulse might be to go for a higher return and ignore your discomfort in regard to the risk. But I think that's a mistake. If you're torn between the desire for return and the desire for stability or safety, my advice is to choose an allocation that will keep your risk at a comfortable level.

There are two main reasons for this. First, remember that the figures in the table are not predictions of the future, only hypothetical results from the past. And the past is a more reliable indicator of risk than it is of returns. In other words, for any given combination of assets, the pattern of volatility is likely to be more predictable than the pattern of return.

I believe the long-term returns from 1970 through 2010 are reasonable to expect in the future. For example, in the 44 years from 1926 through 1969, the S&P 500 Index had a compound rate of return of 9.8 percent. From 1970 through 2010, the compound return of the index was 10 percent, almost identical to its 1926–1969 "normal" performance.

Second, it is never acceptable or advisable to manage a portfolio in violation of your risk tolerance. Year after year, decade after decade, we see people who learn that lesson the hard way, making it an extremely expensive lesson. They are typically the ones who bail out of their investments near the bottom of a market cycle. They become bitter and cynical about investing. Worse, they often stay out of the markets for many years, sometimes even permanently, for fear of being burned again.

Putting This All Together

If there is only one lesson you take from this appendix, I hope it is this: Never ignore your emotions or your "better judgment" in order to chase higher returns. It's just not worth it. When we talk to clients who need or want higher returns than their emotions are likely to tolerate, we spell out a few options, which of course they already know about.

We often recommend that investors settle for lower returns in order to reduce their risks. If you do that while you're still working, you might have to work longer or save more each year before you retire. But that is much better than retiring with too little money. If you are already retired, accepting lower returns might mean you will have less money to spend. Yet that is far better than suffering losses that put you in danger of running out of money.

With education, you may be able to increase your tolerance for risk. But for most of us, risk tolerance or risk aversion is part of who we are and not subject to much change. So unless you are certain that you are comfortable with higher risk, don't chase high returns at the expense of being able to sleep well.

For most people, finding the proper balance between risk and return can be quite challenging. Most investors need the help of a professional advisor to navigate these waters, and in fact this is one of the best reasons I can think of to have an advisor.

Your advisor should be giving you guidance on finding the proper amount of risk in your portfolio. If you're not getting that guidance, ask for it.

How Much in Stocks?

Finding the right ratio of risks to rewards is one of the most important things an investor can do—perhaps more important than anything else. I hope you will take that step.

If you want to see comparable numbers for other equity combinations, you can find them online at Merriman.com (http://www.merriman.com/) in a popular article of the same title as this appendix, "Fine-Tuning Your Asset Allocation." An expanded table in that article shows the results of 41 years of investments allocated between stocks and bonds in 10 percent increments, from 100 percent bonds to 100 percent stocks.

ANNUAL RETURNS OF FOUR ASSET ALLOCATIONS

Equity portion is 50 percent U.S./50 percent International and assumes payment of 1 percent annual management fee

	40% Equity	50% Equity	60% Equity	S&P 500 Index W/Divs
1970	6.4	4.7	2.9	4.0
1971	15.4	17.7	20.0	14.3
1972	12.8	15.1	17.5	19.0
1973	(5.9)	(8.1)	(10.3)	(14.7)
1974	(7.1)	(10.2)	(13.2)	(26.5)
1975	21.8	25.7	29.6	37.2
1976	14.9	16.3	17.6	23.8
1977	11.3	13.8	16.3	(7.2)
1978	12.3	15.3	18.3	6.6
1979	8.7	9.6	10.5	18.4
1980	13.8	16.0	18.2	32.4
1981	6.1	5.4	4.7	(4.9)
1982	19.5	18.3	17.1	21.4
1983	15.8	18.2	20.6	22.5
1984	10.5	9.9	9.2	6.3

continued

ANNUAL RETURNS OF FOUR ASSET ALLOCATIONS (CONTINUED)

Equity portion is 50 percent U.S./50 percent International and assumes payment of 1 percent annual management fee

	40% Equity	50% Equity	60% Equity	S&P 500 Index W/Divs
1985	26.0	28.3	30.6	32.2
1986	21.1	23.3	25.6	18.5
1987	8.8	10.4	11.9	5.2
1988	13.3	15.3	17.3	16.8
1989	16.4	17.4	18.5	31.5
1990	(1.1)	(3.4)	(5.7)	(3.1)
1991	19.7	21.1	22.5	30.5
1992	5.3	5.0	4.7	7.6
1993	16.4	18.4	20.3	10.1
1994	(1.8)	(1.1)	(0.4)	1.3
1995	15.8	15.8	15.8	37.6
1996	6.4	7.5	8.6	23.0
1997	5.9	5.7	5.6	33.4
1998	6.4	6.0	5.6	28.6
1999	7.0	9.2	11.5	21.0
2000	5.3	3.9	2.6	(9.1)
2001	3.7	2.9	1.9	(11.9)
2002	3.9	1.8	(0.3)	(22.1)
2003	19.2	23.6	28.2	28.7
2004	11.1	13.2	15.3	10.9
2005	5.8	7.0	8.3	4.9
2006	10.5	12.7	14.9	15.8
2007	6.1	5.4	4.8	5.5
2008	(14.8)	(19.8)	(24.5)	(37.0)
2009	15.4	19.0	22.6	26.5
2010	11.3	12.8	14.4	15.1
Annualized Return	9.4	10.0	10.6	10.0
Standard Deviation	7.0	8.2	9.6	15.7
Worst Month	(10.7)	(12.8)	(14.9)	(21.5)
Worst 12 Months	(23.1)	(28.5)	(33.5)	(43.3)
Worst 60 Months	1.6	(2.7)	(7.0)	(29.1)

APPENDIX C
The Ultimate
Buy-and-Hold Strategy

This appendix shows how a series of simple but powerful concepts can benefit patient, thoughtful investors of all ages.

If you are a serious investor, this could be one of the most important things you'll ever read. This outlines an investment strategy that I've been recommending for more than 15 years. I still think so highly of it that I call it the Ultimate Buy-and-Hold Strategy.

I don't claim this is the best investment strategy in the world, but it's the best one I have found, and I believe almost every long-term investor can put it to good use.

Compared with the U.S. stock market as measured by the Standard & Poor's 500 Index, the Ultimate Buy-and-Hold Strategy has historically increased returns and reduced risk. This strategy is suitable for do-it-yourself investors as well as those who use professional investment advisors. It works in small portfolios and large portfolios. It's easy to understand and easy to apply using low-cost no-load mutual funds.

I didn't invent this strategy. It has evolved over a long period from the work of many people, including some winners and nominees for the Nobel Prize in economics.

Setting a High Standard

In theory, a perfect investment strategy would be cheap, easy, and risk free. It would make you fabulously rich in about a week—without any tax obligation, of course. I haven't found that combination, and I don't expect to find it. But in the real world, this is the closest thing I know.

Over the long run, the Ultimate Buy-and-Hold Strategy has produced higher returns than the investments many people hold. It did so at less risk, with minimal transaction costs. It's mechanical, so it doesn't require you to pore over newsletters, pick stocks, find a guru, or understand the economy.

This Strategy in a Nutshell

Even though this strategy is based on academic research, it's really fairly simple. If I had to describe it in a single sentence, I would say that the Ultimate Buy-and-Hold Strategy uses low-cost no-load funds to create a sophisticated asset allocation model with worldwide equity diversification by adding value stocks, small-company stocks, and real estate funds to a traditional large-cap growth stock portfolio.

If you think you already know what that means and you're tempted to skip the rest of this explanation and go straight to the recommendations, I hope you'll resist that temptation. I have some compelling evidence to show you. If you apply this diligently, doing so could make a big difference in your future and your family's future.

If there is a "catch" to this strategy, it's availability. You cannot buy it in a single mutual fund. You can put together most of it using Vanguard's low-cost index funds; but Vanguard doesn't offer every piece of it. If you use more than one fund family and include exchange-traded funds (ETFs), you can get each individual piece. But in order to do that you may have to open more than a single investment account, and you might have to pay more in expenses than I would regard as ideal.

What Really Matters

The Ultimate Buy-and-Hold Strategy is based on more than 50 years of research into a deceptively simple question: What really makes a difference to investors?

Some of the answers may surprise you. The people behind this research include Harry Markowitz, a 1990 Nobel laureate; Rex A. Sinquefield, who started the first index fund; and Eugene F. Fama, Robert R. McCormick Distinguished Service Professor of Finance at the University of Chicago Booth School of Business.

Their expertise is pooled in a company that Sinquefield and David Booth started in 1981 in order to give institutional investors a practical way to take advantage of their research. Today, that company, Dimensional Fund Advisors, manages more than $180 billion of investments for pension funds, large corporations, and a family of terrific mutual funds that are available to the public through a select group of investment advisors.

Not for Everybody

Before we get into the meat of this strategy, there are a few things you should know. Every investment and every investment strategy involves risks, both short term and long term. That means investors can always lose money. The Ultimate Buy-and-Hold Strategy is not suitable for every investment need. It won't necessarily do well every week, every month, every quarter, or every year. As investors learned the hard way in 2007 and 2008, there will be times when it loses money. You have been warned.

Like most worthwhile ways to invest, this strategy requires investors to make a commitment. If you are the sort of investor who dabbles in a strategy to check it out for a quarter or two, don't even bother with this. You will be disappointed, and you'll be relying entirely on luck for such short-term results.

I am often asked how this strategy did last year or how it's doing so far this year. Some people tell me they think investors should be in some particular kind of asset over the next few months or the next year. Almost always, this is the result of something they have read or heard without checking it out thoroughly on their own. These people aren't likely to succeed with this strategy because they are focused on the short term.

The Ultimate Buy-and-Hold Strategy is not based on anything that happened last year or last quarter. It's not based on anything that is expected to happen next quarter or next year. It makes absolutely no attempt to identify what investments will be "hot" in the near future. If that's what you want, you should look elsewhere because you won't find it here.

This strategy is designed to produce results that are very long term without requiring much maintenance. If that is what you want, you are in the right place.

The Assets Make the Difference

The most important building block of this strategy is your choice of assets. Many investors think success lies in buying and selling at exactly the right times or in finding the right gurus or managers, the right stocks, or the right mutual funds. But being at the right place at the right time depends on luck, and luck can work against you just as much as for you.

Here's the truth: Your choice of asset classes has far more impact on your results than any other investment decision you will make. I know this advice flies in the face of a lot of conventional wisdom and almost all the marketing hype on Wall Street, so I want to repeat it. Your choice of the right assets is far more important than exactly when you buy or sell those assets. And it's much more important than finding the very "best" stocks, bonds, or mutual funds.

In a 1986 study that is often cited by investment managers and that was largely confirmed by a follow-up study five years later, researchers tracked the investments of 91 large pension funds from 1974 to 1983. They concluded that more than 93 percent of the variation in returns could be attributed to the kinds of assets in the portfolio. Most of the remaining variation was due to stock picking and the timing of purchases and sales.

Basic Building Blocks

So how do you choose the right asset classes? I'll use a series of pie charts (reprinted with permission from Merriman, Inc.) to show you how, starting with Portfolio One, a very basic investment mix. Assume the whole pie represents all the money you have invested. Portfolio One's pie has only two slices, one for bonds (Barclay's Govt. Credit Index) and one for equities (Standard & Poor's 500 Index).

The returns cited here do *not* reflect the transaction costs, fees, and expenses that investors must inevitably pay. These figures represent the returns of asset classes, not specific investments.

Portfolio One's 60/40 split between stocks and bonds is the way that pension funds, insurance companies, and other large institutional investors have traditionally allocated their assets. The stocks provide long-term growth while the bonds provide stability and income.

PORTFOLIO ONE January 1970–December 2010

	Annualized Return	Annualized Standard Deviation
Portfolio One	9.6%	11.9%

$100,000 grew to $4,272,337

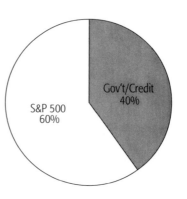

Gov't/Credit 40%

S&P 500 60%

Let me say up front that we don't believe 60 percent stocks and 40 percent bonds is the right balance for all investors. Many young investors don't need any bonds in their portfolios. And many older folks may want 70 percent or more of their portfolios in bonds. However, the 60/40 ratio of Portfolio One is a good long-term investment mix. It's an industry standard, and I'll use it here to illustrate my points.

In the 41 years from January 1970 through December 2010, this portfolio produced a compound annual return of 9.6 percent. That's not bad, especially considering this period included four major bear markets. I believe that return should be more than enough to let most investors achieve their long-term goals.

Therefore, for this discussion I will use a long-term annual return of 9.6 percent as a benchmark against which to measure the strategy I'm presenting. You'll see this strategy unfold as we split the pie into thinner and thinner slices by adding asset classes.

Remember that we also must look at risk. We want risk to remain the same—or ideally, to decline. Therefore, another measure I'll use to gauge this strategy is standard deviation.

Standard deviation is a statistical way to measure risk. (If you want to understand this statistically, there are plenty of resources online that will tell you how it's defined and applied.) For our purposes here, it's enough to know that a lower number is better, indicating a portfolio that is more predictable and less volatile. The standard deviation of Portfolio One is 11.9 percent, so we'll use that as the benchmark.

The evidence is overwhelming that historically, millions of investors would have been better off with Portfolio One than they were with their actual portfolios, which typically included too little diversification and too much risk. If those investors did nothing more than adopt this simple mix of assets—which is easily duplicated using a couple of no-load index funds, they would be more likely to achieve their long-term investment goals.

Because of that, and because it is used by institutional investors who must get the equation right for the long term, I believe Portfolio One is a relatively high standard from which to start. In my view, anything worthy of being called an "ultimate" strategy must beat Portfolio One in two ways. It must be worthy of a reasonable expectation that it will produce a return higher than 9.6 percent and at the same time have a standard deviation of 11.9 percent or less.

Most of the Ultimate Buy-and-Hold Strategy is concerned with the 60 percent equity side of the pie. That's where the main focus is here. But it's very important to get the bond part of this strategy right.

Most people include bond funds in a portfolio in order to provide stability, which can be measured by standard deviation. Many investors also expect bond funds to produce income, which of course is part of any investor's total return. The more bonds a portfolio has, the lower its long-term expected return and the lower its risk. The more stocks a portfolio has, the higher its long-term expected return and the higher the level of risk. This relationship does not hold true over every period, but in the very long term, the pattern has been consistent.

Getting Bonds Right

Whether your portfolio is heavy or light on bonds, it matters what kind of bonds you own. In general, longer bond maturities go together with higher yields and higher volatility (higher standard deviation, in other words). However, as you extend maturities beyond intermediate-term bonds, the added volatility (risk) rises much faster than the additional return.

Our recommended bond portfolio is exclusively in government fixed-income funds and is comprised of 50 percent intermediate-term funds, 30 percent short-term funds, and 20 percent in Treasury inflation-protected securities (TIPS) funds for inflation protection. (TIPS funds invest in U.S. Treasury inflation-protected securities, which automatically adjust their values and interest payments to changes in the Consumer Price Index.)

We exclude corporate bond funds because they entail some risk of default—a risk that tends to increase at the very times when we want stability the most. We believe in taking calculated risks on the stock side of the portfolio and being very conservative on the fixed-income side. U.S. Treasury securities are the safest in the world and virtually eliminate the risk of default.

Making these changes gives us Portfolio Two. From 1970 through 2010, this combination had an annualized return of 9.6 percent and a standard deviation of 11.3 percent. This change gives the portfolio more stability (less risk) at the same return.

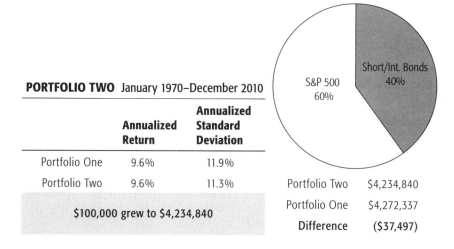

PORTFOLIO TWO January 1970–December 2010

	Annualized Return	Annualized Standard Deviation
Portfolio One	9.6%	11.9%
Portfolio Two	9.6%	11.3%

$100,000 grew to $4,234,840

Portfolio Two	$4,234,840
Portfolio One	$4,272,337
Difference	($37,497)

The improvement over Portfolio One is modest, a tiny reduction of return over 41 years coupled with a reduction of risk. But there's much more to come as we tackle the 60 percent of the portfolio devoted to equities.

Getting Equities Right: Adding Real Estate

Despite recent history, investors are familiar with the long-term attraction of owning real estate. When this asset class is owned through professionally managed real estate investment trusts known as REITs, it can reduce risk and increase return.

From 1975 through 2010, REITs compounded at 14 percent, outpacing the Standard & Poor's 500 Index (which returned 11.8 percent over that same period). This was an unusually productive period for REITs, and academic researchers expect the future returns of real estate and of the S&P 500 Index to be similar to each other—though not as high as they were during this period.

As you can see in Portfolio Three, when REITs made up one-fifth of the stock part of this portfolio, the annual return rose slightly, to 9.9 percent; more important for our purposes, the standard deviation (risk) fell to 10.6 percent. At this point we have accomplished our objective of adding return and reducing risk. Over this long period, the bottom line is an additional $451,245 in cumulative return. This is an excellent start, but the best is still to come.

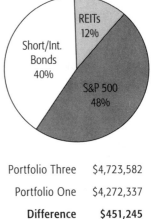

PORTFOLIO THREE January 1970–December 2010

	Annualized Return	Annualized Standard Deviation
Portfolio One	9.6%	11.9%
Portfolio Two	9.6%	11.3%
Portfolio Three	9.9%	10.6%

$100,000 grew to $4,723,582

Portfolio Three	$4,723,582
Portfolio One	$4,272,337
Difference	$451,245

Getting Equities Right: Size Matters

The standard pension fund's stock portfolio, reflected here in Portfolios One and Two, consists mostly of the stocks of the 500 largest U.S. companies. These include many familiar names like Exxon Mobil, General Electric, Johnson & Johnson, Microsoft, Pfizer, and Procter & Gamble. Each of these was once a small company going through rapid growth that paid off in a big way for early investors. Microsoft was a classic case in the 1980s and 1990s.

Because small companies can grow much faster than huge ones, a fundamental way to diversify a stock portfolio is to invest some of your money in stocks of small companies.

To accomplish this, the next step in building the Ultimate Buy-and-Hold Strategy is to add small-company stocks to the equity part of the portfolio. To represent these stocks, we have used the returns of the Dimensional Fund Advisors U.S. Micro Cap Fund, which invests in the smallest 5 percent of U.S. companies.

The result is Portfolio Four, a pie that now has four slices. From 1970 through 2010, this combination produced an annualized return of 10.1 percent, with a standard deviation of 11 percent. With these three changes, we added about $947,000 to the cumulative return, an increase of 22.2 percent.

Stop for a moment and think about that. I've just described a couple of simple steps that added additional return that's more than seven times the entire initial investment of $100,000.

How much work did it take to capture that extra return? I'm betting you could set this up with less than 20 hours of your time. But let's be conservative and say that it took you 40 hours, a full standard workweek. Divide the extra return by those hours and the payoff amounts to about $23,000 per hour. I don't know anywhere else you can get paid that much for your time. If you do, I hope you'll let me know! Could I now interest you in doubling that extra return without adding more hours?

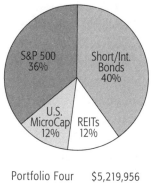

PORTFOLIO FOUR January 1970–December 2010

	Annualized Return	Annualized Standard Deviation
Portfolio One	9.6%	11.9%
Portfolio Two	9.6%	11.3%
Portfolio Three	9.9%	10.6%
Portfolio Four	10.1%	11.0%

$100,000 grew to $5,219,956

Portfolio Four	$5,219,956
Portfolio One	$4,272,337
Difference	$947,619

Getting Equities Right: Adding Value

The next step is to differentiate between what are known as growth stocks and value stocks. Typical growth investors look for companies with rising sales and profits, companies that either dominate their markets or seem to be on the brink of doing so. These companies are typical of those in the S&P 500 Index of Portfolio One.

Value investors, on the other hand, look for companies that for one reason or another may be temporary bargains. They may be out of favor with big investors because of things like poor management, weak finances, new competition, or problems with unions, government agencies, and defective products.

Value stocks are regarded as bargains that are expected to return to their supposedly "normal" levels when the market perceives their prospects more positively. Some well-known examples, taken from the largest holdings of the Vanguard Value Index Fund in the summer of 2011, include JPMorgan Chase, Procter & Gamble, General Electric, AT&T, and Chevron.

The Ultimate Buy-and-Hold Strategy uses a purely mechanical approach to identify value companies. This approach starts by identifying the largest 50 percent of stocks traded on the New York Stock Exchange and then including all other public companies of similar size. These companies are then sorted by the ratio of their price per share to their book value per share. The top 30 percent of this list, the companies with the highest price-to-book ratios, are classified as large-cap growth companies. The companies in the bottom 30 percent are classified as large-cap value companies. The process is the same for small-cap stocks.

Although the most popular stocks are growth stocks, much research shows that historically, unpopular (value) stocks outperform popular (growth) stocks. This is true of large-company stocks and small-company stocks, and it's true of international stocks as well. From 1927 through 2010, an index of large U.S. growth stocks produced an annualized return of 7.6 percent; large U.S. value stocks, by contrast, had a comparable return of 10.7 percent. Among small-cap stocks over the same period, growth stocks returned 8.2 percent, and value stocks returned 13.3 percent.

Therefore, we create Portfolio Five by adding slices of large-cap value and small-cap value so that the equity side of the portfolio is divided equally five ways.

This boosts the portfolio's historic return to 11 percent, still with a slightly lower standard deviation than Portfolio One. I hope you will notice how much this adds to the 41-year cumulative return: nearly $3 million, or more than three times the "added value" that came from Portfolio Four.

To recap, we started with a standard industry portfolio mix, refined the fixed-income portion, and added real estate, small-cap, and value stocks to the equity portion. The result is an increase of nearly 15 percent in annualized return (and of about 69 percent in cumulative return) at essentially the same level of risk.

Now there is one more very important step in creating the Ultimate Buy-and-Hold Strategy.

Getting Equities Right Globally

The final step toward Portfolio Six takes us beyond the borders of the United States to invest in international stocks. Indexes of U.S. and international stocks often go up and down at different times and different

PORTFOLIO FIVE January 1970–December 2010

	Annualized Return	Annualized Standard Deviation
Portfolio One	9.6%	11.9%
Portfolio Two	9.6%	11.3%
Portfolio Three	9.9%	10.6%
Portfolio Four	10.1%	11.0%
Portfolio Five	11.0%	11.8%

$100,000 grew to $7,234,646

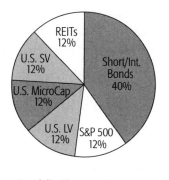

Portfolio Five	$7,234,646
Portfolio One	$4,272,337
Difference	$2,962,310

speeds. Because of this, international stocks are diversifiers that can reduce volatility. However, U.S. and international stocks can decline at the same time, as we saw in 2008.

Like U.S. stocks, international stocks have a long-term upward bias. Yet when the shorter-term movements of U.S. and international stock markets offset each other, as they often do, the combination has a smoother long-term upward curve than either one by itself.

There are two major reasons international stocks help diversify U.S. stocks. First, they trade and operate in different economic environments with different growth rates and monetary policies. Second, currency fluctuations affect their prices when translated into U.S. dollars.

The virtues of small-company stocks and value stocks apply equally to international stocks as to U.S. stocks. Portfolio Six slices the equity portion equally 10 ways, adding international large, international large value, international small, international small value, and emerging markets stocks.

Emerging markets stocks have outperformed the Standard & Poor's 500 Index over long periods of time. They represent countries that are growing rapidly, and they have become an increasingly important part of the world's total market capital.

As you'll see, the annualized return of Portfolio Six jumps to 12.1 percent and the standard deviation is 11.8 percent. Cumulatively over 41 years, this portfolio grew to $10.6 million, more than twice as much as Portfolio One. If you go back to my premise that you could implement this strategy in a total of 40 hours, the added-value return works out to about $158,000 per hour for your time. (Too bad you can't do that for a whole career!)

This completes the basic makeup of the Ultimate Buy-and-Hold Strategy, which over this time period increased annualized return by

PORTFOLIO SIX January 1970–December 2010

	Annualized Return	Annualized Standard Deviation
Portfolio One	9.6%	11.9%
Portfolio Two	9.6%	11.3%
Portfolio Three	9.9%	10.6%
Portfolio Four	10.1%	11.0%
Portfolio Five	11.0%	11.8%
Portfolio Six	12.1%	11.8%

$100,000 grew to $10,621,847

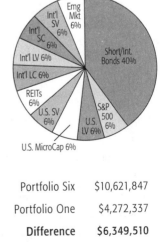

Portfolio Six	$10,621,847
Portfolio One	$4,272,337
Difference	$6,349,510

26 percent without increasing volatility. This investment strategy is not complicated, and it's based on solid research, not hocus-pocus. It doesn't require a guru. It doesn't require investors to figure out the economic landscape or predict the future.

Putting This Strategy to Work

As I mentioned earlier, there's no single mutual fund that puts all the pieces of this together under one roof. For help in finding funds, I recommend Appendix D, "The Best Mutual Funds."

A Note on Using This Strategy in
Taxable Accounts

This combination of asset classes works best in tax-sheltered accounts such as individual retirement accounts (IRAs) and company retirement plans. In taxable accounts, we recommend leaving out the REIT fund and dividing that portion of the portfolio equally among the other four U.S. equity classes. I say this because real estate funds produce much of their total return in the form of income dividends that do not qualify for the favorable tax treatment afforded to most other dividends.

Many investors implement this strategy in taxable accounts to supplement their employee retirement plans in order to capture asset classes not available in those plans. Investors who take this approach, which we favor, should hold REIT funds in their tax-sheltered accounts.

What's Wrong with This Strategy

Even though this is the best long-term buy-and-hold strategy that I know, it isn't flawless. Investment markets are not highly predictable, and this strategy might not work as well in the future as it did in the past.

The stock side of this portfolio is overweighted to value stocks, and it is quite possible that value stocks will underperform growth stocks over the next 5, 10, 15, or 20 years. The portfolio also contains lots of small-company stocks. But it's possible that large-company stocks will do better than small ones in the future. This portfolio contains more exposure to international stocks than most advisors recommend. International stocks could underperform U.S. stocks in the future. Likewise, it's possible that bonds, which make up only 40 percent of this portfolio, could do better than stocks in the future.

Nevertheless, I believe the Ultimate Buy-and-Hold Strategy deals very well with these uncertainties. If you own this portfolio, you aren't dependent on any particular asset class. You have them all. And no matter which ones are doing well, you will own them.

To my mind, this is the best an investor can do. And when you have done your best, it's time to turn your attention to something else. A good place to start is by making sure you are living your life the way you want to.

APPENDIX D
The Best Mutual Funds

I have been teaching investors how to use Vanguard and Dimensional Fund Advisors funds for more than a decade. Here I'll show how they compare.

The most important favor that long-term investors can do for themselves is to invest in the right kinds of assets, or asset classes. Examples of asset classes are stocks and bonds. More specific examples are U.S. large-company value stocks, emerging markets stocks, high-yield bonds, and short-term corporate bonds.

Dimensional Fund Advisors, a mutual fund company in Santa Monica, California, studied the returns of 44 institutional pension funds with about $450 billion in assets over various time periods averaging nine years. The study concluded that more than 96 percent of the variation in returns could be attributed to the kinds of assets in the portfolios. Most of the remaining 4 percent was attributable to stock picking and the timing of purchases and sales.

Stated another way, 96 percent of investing is about understanding the job that needs to be done. The other 4 percent is about picking the very best tools to get that job done. Do this right, and you're most of the way there. Do this wrong, and at best your money is not working hard for you. At worst, you're taking too much risk, and you could get clobbered by the market.

Ironically, most investors spend most of their time on the decisions that make just 4 percent of the difference and very little time on decisions that make 96 percent of the difference.

That is not to say that the 4 percent is inconsequential. The opposite is true, as we shall see, and this appendix is about that 4 percent. Once you understand asset allocation and know which asset classes you need, you should find the most efficient, lowest-cost, least-risky, and most productive mutual funds for your money.

There are lots of places you can invest your money and get an adequate return. But if you're investing for a long time, you should hold out for great investments instead of settling for those that are merely good enough.

I'm going to compare and contrast two families of excellent low-cost no-load mutual funds that do a lot of seemingly small things right: Vanguard and Dimensional Fund Advisors.

You're probably familiar with Vanguard, which is known for its index funds and for cutting its expenses to the bone. Vanguard is our favorite fund family for investors who don't hire advisors to manage their assets. Vanguard funds are suitable for investors of all ages and all levels of wealth.

Dimensional Fund Advisors funds have some important advantages over Vanguard, and I believe those advantages over time could mean an extra one to two percentage points of annualized return.

Little Things Add Up

How significant is an extra return of one to two percentage points annually?

Imagine a working couple adding $10,000 to a pair of Roth IRAs every year for 30 years. If they eliminate commissions, minimize their ongoing expenses, and find ways to invest in just the right asset classes, it's not unreasonable to think they could increase their expected long-term return from 8 percent to 10 percent without taking more overall risk.

Over 30 years, this imaginary couple would have invested a total of $300,000. At the end of that time, an 8 percent return would make their IRAs worth about $1.2 million. At 10 percent, the IRAs would be worth about $1.8 million. The difference is about twice as much as the total of all the money they put into the accounts.

That is a very big difference.

Dimensional Fund Advisors has attracted a huge amount of money, much of it from big institutional investors, on the strength of the many small things they do very well. I'm going to walk you through some of those things, one at a time, comparing Dimensional funds with the comparable funds offered by Vanguard. In addition, we show how both sets of funds compare with their category averages as compiled by Morningstar Inc. The tables that follow are reprinted with permission from Merriman, Inc.

The Funds

The table that follows lists the specific funds I'll be discussing, along with their ticker symbols to let you look them up and find more information on them whenever you like.

One thing you may notice is that Vanguard has no international small-company value fund. This is an important asset class that has helped many diversified portfolios during some serious bear markets when most U.S. stock funds were languishing or worse. Vanguard's portfolio is weaker in this comparison because the company does not offer this asset class in a mutual fund.

(In our recommendations to investors, we have replaced Vanguard International Explorer Fund with Vanguard FTSE All World ex-U.S. Small Cap Index Fund. But that fund has a limited track record, and for purposes of this comparison we are using International Explorer.)

RECOMMENDED DFA AND VANGUARD FUNDS

Fund	Ticker	Fund	Ticker
DFA U.S. Large Company	DFLCX	Vanguard 500 Index	VFINX
DFA U.S. Large-Cap Value	DFLVX	Vanguard Value Index	VIVAX
DFA U.S. Micro Cap	DFSCX	Vanguard Small-Cap Index	NAESX
DFA U.S. Small-Cap Value	DFSVX	Vanguard Small-Cap Value Index	VISVX
DFA U.S. REITs	DFREX	Vanguard REIT Index	VGSIX
DFA International Large Cap	DFALX	Vanguard Developed Markets	VDMIX
DFA International Large-Cap Value	DFIVX	Vanguard International Value	VTRIX
DFA International Small Cap	DFISX	Vanguard International Explorer	VINEX
DFA International Small-Cap Value	DISVX	(none)	
DFA Emerging Markets Core Equity	DFCEX	Vanguard Emerging Markets	VEIEX

Expenses

After asset allocation, the most reliable predictor of investment success is reducing expenses. Savvy investors know that every dollar they pay in expenses is a dollar they won't ever see again, a dollar that will never earn more money for them. On the other hand, every dollar that remains in your portfolio is working for you instead of fattening somebody else's wallet.

Obviously, expenses are inevitable in investing. No company will create and manage portfolios for you, keep records of your account, and provide statements and customer service for free. These are legitimate expenses, and you should expect to pay for them. However, some companies charge much less for them than others.

The following table shows the annual expense ratios for the Dimensional funds and the Vanguard funds that are listed in the previous table. You'll see that both fund families charge expenses far below the Morningstar category averages. Both funds' expenses are very low, and Vanguard's are lower than those of Dimensional.

Despite their slightly higher expenses, I still regard Dimensional funds as the best that I know. Their superiority is not the result of having better managers picking better stocks. This edge comes from precise asset allocation that gives investors more of what they need and less of what they don't need.

MUTUAL FUND EXPENSE RATIOS

Asset Class	Dimensional	Vanguard	Category Average
U.S. large cap	0.10%	0.18%	1.12%
U.S. large-cap value	0.30%	0.26%	1.27%
U.S. small cap	0.40%	0.28%	1.41%
U.S. small-cap value	0.54%	0.28%	1.48%
U.S. REITs	0.36%	0.26%	1.49%
International large cap	0.32%	0.10%	1.39%
International large-cap value	0.46%	0.45%	1.39%
International small cap	0.57%	0.45%	1.58%
International small-cap value	0.71%		1.52%
Emerging markets	0.67%	0.40%	1.74%
Average	**0.44%**	**0.30%**	**1.44%**

What investors need in the long run is diversification in addition to the ever-popular large-company growth stocks that clog so many portfolios. For reasons that I have described at length in Appendix C, "The Ultimate Buy-and-Hold Strategy," investors have benefited a lot through the years from including stocks of smaller companies and of value companies in their portfolios.

To get this diversification, we look for value funds that have a stronger orientation to value and for small-cap funds that hold smaller companies. Dimensional funds, in each case, deliver the goods.

Size Matters

To evaluate a mutual fund properly, you need to study exactly what's in its portfolio.

Size is very important, and it's very easy to measure. Every public company has a total market capitalization, the theoretical value that investors collectively assign to the whole company. This is calculated by multiplying the share price times the total number of shares.

Large-cap companies like General Electric have market capitalizations of more than $110 billion. Many companies you have never heard of have total market capitalizations of less than $100 million.

The following table, on the next page, shows the average market capitalization of the portfolios of the 19 Dimensional and Vanguard funds. Remembering that smaller is better in a small-cap value fund, consider the two funds in that category. Dimensional fund's portfolio has an average market capitalization of $676 million. The Vanguard fund's comparable figure is more than $1.2 billion—above the industry average.

You will see there's not much difference between Dimensional and Vanguard in the average market capitalizations of their U.S. and international large-cap blend funds and their real estate funds. But in every other category, the difference is quite striking, and the averages reflect that.

Vanguard has an excellent emerging markets fund. But large and giant companies (as defined by Morningstar) make up about 76 percent of that portfolio. Large and giant companies make up about 57 percent of the Dimensional emerging markets fund. To state this another way, Dimensional's fund leaves 43 percent of its portfolio for mid-cap and small-cap companies; Vanguard leaves only about 24 percent.

AVERAGE MARKET CAPITALIZATION (IN MILLIONS)

Asset Class	Dimensional	Vanguard	Category Average
U.S. large cap	$43,644	$44,133	$31,795
U.S. large-cap value	$23,200	$37,645	$33,584
U.S. small cap	$801	$1,285	$1,202
U.S. small-cap value	$717	$1,271	$1,135
U.S. REITs	$5,533	$5,255	$5,351
International large cap	$29,366	$29,421	$23,422
International large-cap value	$20,341	$33,705	$24,737
International small cap	$972	$1,433	$2,348
International small-cap value	$924		$2,331
Emerging markets	$7,774	$18,231	$14,868
Average	**$13,329**	**$19,153**	**$14,077**

This is an example of easily overlooked details that can add up to meaningful differences in performance.

Value

Over the long run, investors have earned higher returns from value companies than from growth companies.

Value is trickier to quantify than size. Many investors regard value companies as those that are out of favor and perhaps ripe for turn-arounds. That's the sort of value definition that Wall Street likes because it emphasizes the role of smart stock-picking and implies a need to pay for experts who can identify companies with the most future potential.

However, academic experts demand a more objective approach. The generally accepted measure of a value company is its price-to-book ratio, often abbreviated as price/book. This is the current price of the stock divided by the book value per share. Book value is the total of all assets minus all liabilities on the company's books divided by the number of shares.

Book value emphasizes corporate assets. Manufacturing companies with huge investments in plants and equipment will often have relatively high book values.

At the opposite end of the scale, growth companies may rely more on the brains of their employees. Those brains are very real assets, but they don't have price tags, they don't technically belong to the companies, and as some analysts love to say, those assets "walk out the door every night."

Growth companies tend to have lower book values and thus higher price/book ratios. Investors in Google, Apple, and Microsoft aren't relying on manufacturing plants and office buildings; they're relying on brainpower and patents and creativity.

I don't advocate investing in value companies one by one. I believe in owning them by the hundreds and even by the thousands. That's easy to do by investing in value funds.

It stands to reason then that a value fund should have an average price/book ratio that's lower than most other funds. The lower that ratio, the stronger the value orientation.

The following table shows the average price/book ratios of portfolios in Dimensional and Vanguard funds.

I believe those numbers are important in understanding why most Dimensional funds had better performance than the corresponding Vanguard funds in the most recent 10-year period. These were years in which value stocks and small-company stocks performed better than growth stocks and large-company stocks.

In the past, those patterns have held true over long periods of time. But there are periods when growth stocks do better and when large

VALUE ORIENTATION: AVERAGE PRICE/BOOK RATIOS IN MUTUAL FUNDS

Asset Class	Dimensional	Vanguard	Category Average
U.S. large cap	2.1	2.1	2.0
U.S. large-cap value	1.2	1.5	1.7
U.S. small cap	1.7	1.7	1.7
U.S. small-cap value	1.0	1.3	1.3
U.S. REITs	2.0	2.0	2.0
International large cap	1.5	1.5	1.7
International large-cap value	1.0	1.4	1.4
International small cap	1.2	1.5	1.7
International small-cap value	0.7		1.3
Emerging markets	1.8	2.2	2.3
Average	**1.4**	**1.7**	**1.7**

stocks do better. In those times, some Dimensional funds will lag their Vanguard counterparts.

Portfolio Turnover

When I look "under the hood" at a portfolio I always like to peek at portfolio turnover. You may be a buy-and-hold investor, but your fund manager could be a trader, driving up transaction costs that eat away at returns in addition to the expense ratios we looked at earlier.

The following table shows the annual percentage turnover in the funds we're comparing. Note that both Vanguard and Dimensional have much lower average turnover than the category averages. The two U.S. large-cap funds turned over no more than 12 percent of their portfolios in a year, compared with 77 percent in the average fund in the category.

ANNUAL PORTFOLIO TURNOVER (IN PERCENT)

Asset Class	Dimensional	Vanguard	Category Average
U.S. large cap	10	12	77
U.S. large-cap value	29	31	64
U.S. small cap	17	14	80
U.S. small-cap value	21	33	75
U.S. REITs	2	16	128
International large cap	12	14	92
International large-cap value	18	55	65
International small cap	13	52	81
International small-cap value	22		65
Emerging markets	6	12	85
Average	**15**	**27**	**81**

Reducing Risk Through Diversification

For a final peek into the details of what these funds own, I call your attention to the following table, showing portfolio diversification. I believe that over the long term, investors will continue to get premium returns for taking carefully controlled risks. Investing in many companies is less risky than investing in a few companies.

NUMBER OF STOCKS IN FUND PORTFOLIOS

Asset Class	Dimensional	Vanguard	Category Average
U.S. large cap	501	506	208
U.S. large-cap value	212	424	112
U.S. small cap	2,685	1,732	392
U.S. small-cap value	1,529	990	241
U.S. REITs	108	101	70
International large cap	1,302	987	287
International large-cap value	544	250	173
International small cap	4,609	377	364
International small-cap value	2,183		520
Emerging markets	3,204	822	212
Average	**1,688**	**688**	**258**

The table shows that Dimensional funds hold far more companies in their portfolios than the comparable Vanguard funds, especially in U.S. and international funds that invest in small-cap, small-cap value, and emerging markets stocks. This is desirable.

The Proof of the Pudding

The proof, of course, is in the results, as you'll see in the following table, on the next page, which shows returns for the 10 years ended December 31, 2010. Vanguard funds did a bit better than the category average. But Dimensional funds did considerably better, adding two percentage points of return.

Dimensional was founded in 1981 to bring the benefits of academic research to insurance companies, pension funds, and other institutions. The company's mutual funds pinpoint the most productive asset classes and make them available not only to institutions but to some individual investors. Notice the word *some* in that last sentence.

Dimensional funds are available through selected investment advisors that have been approved by Dimensional. Most such advisors charge management fees, typically 1 percent per year, and impose minimum size requirements for opening accounts. Despite those hurdles, I

**ANNUALIZED RETURN OF MUTUAL FUNDS FOR 10 YEARS
ENDING DECEMBER 2010**

Asset Class	Dimensional	Vanguard	Category Average
U.S. large cap	1.4%	1.3%	1.6%
U.S. large-cap value	5.3%	2.0%	3.1%
U.S. small cap	8.3%	7.2%	7.2%
U.S. small-cap value	11.1%	8.0%	9.4%
U.S. REITs	10.5%	10.6%	9.6%
International large cap	3.9%	0.8%	3.1%
International large-cap value	7.8%	6.0%	4.4%
International small cap	11.7%	8.2%	8.3%
International small-cap value	13.5%		9.0%
Emerging markets	18.0%	15.4%	14.9%
Average	**9.2%**	**7.3%**	**7.1%**

believe that over time Dimensional funds will provide the extra edge that will make a great portfolio, not merely a good one.

Saying No to Hot Money

I'm often asked why these funds aren't available to everybody who wants to invest in them. Dimensional funds are based on academic research that assumes long-term holding periods and a strict buy-and-hold approach. That is contrary to typical investor behavior.

Many investors buy and sell based on their emotions and swings in the market. This can create massive inflows and outflows for mutual funds, whose managers can be forced to sell stocks in order to meet redemptions. Typically that occurs when stock prices have been falling; this, in turn, forces fund managers to sell when prices are relatively weak.

Likewise, large cash inflows can force funds either to risk paying too much for stocks as their buying drives up prices or to leave new money in cash, where it is relatively unproductive. Either scenario is likely to reduce returns for all shareholders, and Dimensional simply isn't interested in doing that.

One other point is worth noting. There is no financial arrangement between Dimensional Fund Advisors and any of the advisors who use the company's funds. Dimensional advisors are free to recommend any funds they want to their clients, and they receive no income from Dimensional.

Not Index Funds

Dimensional funds are not index funds. They do not try to exactly match any index, and that's to the shareholders' advantage. A fund that's modeled after the Standard & Poor's 500 Index, for example, is obligated to sell each stock that drops off the index and buy each one that's added to the index—and to do this on the same day that every other S&P 500 Index fund is doing the same thing.

On that particular day, the stocks being sold by all the index funds can be expected to sell for weak prices, since supply will suddenly be greater than demand. At the same time, the stocks being added to all those index funds can be expected to go up in price, reacting to a surge in demand.

Dimensional's U.S. large-cap fund follows the S&P 500 Index closely. But the fund's managers are free to buy and sell when they find more favorable prices. This and other trading strategies allow Dimensional funds to outperform their benchmarks.

What to Do with This Information

If you use a financial advisor, I recommend choosing one who uses Dimensional funds. I believe that over the long term these funds will have an advantage over the equity funds at Vanguard, even after subtracting a presumed 1 percent annual management fee.

If you're accumulating assets over many years, that advantage may make a big difference when you get ready to retire. If you are already retired, I believe that advantage could make the difference between having enough to live comfortably or having to make every penny count.

The Bottom Line

The whole idea of my detailed asset class recommendations is to properly load the stock side of a portfolio with small-company stocks and value stocks. The better job you do of that, the better your long-term results are likely to be.

Unfortunately, you cannot get full diversification using Vanguard funds, though you can come close. Dimensional funds give you the assets that academic research says you need. If there were an equally attractive alternative that didn't require hiring an advisor, I would recommend that alternative.

Obviously, this is your choice. What's at stake is your money and your future. Now you have the information you need to make that choice.

APPENDIX E
Mutual Fund Model Portfolios

I believe millions of mutual fund investors fail to get the full benefits available to them at the fund families they use. If they understood and used their choices better, they could make more money without taking more risk.

In the body of this book (and in more detail in Appendix C, "The Ultimate Buy-and-Hold Strategy"), I have provided the knowledge investors need to make the best fund choices. In the suggested portfolios that follow, I show exactly how to put that knowledge to work at some of the largest mutual fund families in the United States.

Whether you are picking among options in a retirement account managed by one of these companies or shopping for funds in an individual retirement account (IRA) or a taxable account that you manage, the following tables will show you how to gain access to the most important asset classes.

Five Large Mutual Fund Families

In this appendix you will find aggressive, moderate, and conservative recommendations for using the choices available at five large mutual fund families: American Funds, Fidelity, T. Rowe Price, TIAA-CREF, and Vanguard.

You will also find a list of exchange-traded funds (ETFs) you can buy through brokerage accounts. And finally, there's a monthly income portfolio using Vanguard funds.

American Funds

AMERICAN FUNDS MODEL PORTFOLIO SUGGESTED ALLOCATIONS

Fund	Aggressive	Moderate	Conservative
Fundamental Investors	15%	9%	6%
American Mutual	20%	12%	8%
Small-Cap World	25%	15%	10%
EuroPacific Growth	15%	9%	6%
International Growth and Income	15%	9%	6%
New World	10%	6%	4%
U.S. Government Securities	0%	28%	42%
ST Bond Fund of America	0%	12%	18%

I do not recommend American funds, for two reasons. First, their sales loads take assets from investors and give them to salespeople. Second, although many of this company's funds have a commendable tilt toward value stocks, their portfolios do not adhere very tightly to standard asset classes. This makes it difficult, if not impossible, to carefully control the asset allocation of a portfolio composed of the offerings of American funds.

However, millions of investors have assets in American funds, and my goal in this suggested portfolio is to help those investors get the most benefit from their funds.

Fidelity

FIDELITY MODEL PORTFOLIO SUGGESTED ALLOCATIONS

Fund	Aggressive	Moderate	Conservative
Spartan 500 Index	11%	6%	4%
Large-Cap Value Enhanced Index	11%	7%	5%
Small-Cap Enhanced Index	11%	7%	4%
Small-Cap Value	12%	7%	5%
Real Estate Investment	5%	3%	2%
Spartan International Index	9%	6%	3%
International Value	18%	10%	7%
International Small-Cap Opp	9%	5%	4%

Fund	Aggressive	Moderate	Conservative
Emerging Markets	9%	6%	4%
International Real Estate	5%	3%	2%
Intermediate Government Income	0%	20%	30%
Spartan S/T Tr Bond Index	0%	12%	18%
Inflation-Protected Bond	0%	8%	12%

Fidelity's fund lineup, which makes up thousands of 401(k) and similar programs, includes something you won't find at Vanguard or T. Rowe Price—an international real estate fund. This is a valuable asset class, worth including if you can.

T. Rowe Price

T. ROWE PRICE MODEL PORTFOLIO SUGGESTED ALLOCATIONS

Fund	Aggressive	Moderate	Conservative
Equity Index 500	10%	6%	4%
Value	10%	6%	4%
Small-Cap Stock	10%	6%	4%
Small-Cap Value	10%	6%	4%
Real Estate	10%	6%	4%
International Equity Index	10%	6%	4%
International Growth & Income	20%	12%	8%
International Discovery	10%	6%	4%
Emerging Markets Stock	10%	6%	4%
U.S. Treasury Intermediate	0%	20%	30%
Short-Term Bond	0%	12%	18%
Inflation Protected Bond	0%	8%	12%

T. Rowe Price funds are conservatively run and widely available in retirement plans. This company's asset class offerings, like those at Vanguard, lack only international small-company value stocks.

TIAA-CREF

TIAA-CREF MODEL PORTFOLIO SUGGESTED ALLOCATIONS

Fund	Aggressive	Moderate	Conservative
S&P 500 Index	12%	7%	5%
Large-Cap Value Index	13%	8%	5%
Small-Cap Blend Index	25%	15%	10%
Real Estate Securities	10%	6%	4%
International Equity Index	30%	18%	12%
Emerging Markets Index	10%	6%	4%
Bond Index	0%	20%	30%
Short-Term Bond	0%	12%	18%
Inflation-Linked Bond	0%	8%	12%

TIAA-CREF funds are found in the retirement plans at many colleges and universities. The funds don't offer exposure to international value, international small-company, and international small-company value stocks. I am not sure why University Street is willing to accept these limited fund offerings.

Vanguard

VANGUARD MODEL PORTFOLIO SUGGESTED ALLOCATIONS

Fund	Aggressive	Moderate	Conservative
500 Index	10%	6%	4%
Value Index	10%	6%	4%
Small-Cap Index	10%	6%	4%
Small-Cap Value Index	10%	6%	4%
REIT Index	10%	6%	4%
Developed Markets Index	10%	6%	4%
International Value	20%	12%	8%
FTSE All-World ex-U.S. Small-Cap Index	10%	6%	4%
Emerging Markets Stock Index	10%	6%	4%
Intermediate-Term Treasury	0%	20%	30%
Short-Term Treasury	0%	12%	18%
Inflation-Protected Securities	0%	8%	12%

The Vanguard portfolio has all the equity asset classes I recommend except international small-company value stocks. To compensate for that, the international value fund has double the weighting in my recommendations that it would otherwise have. Although this portfolio is listed last for alphabetical reasons, it's my first choice among these families.

ETF

ETF MODEL PORTFOLIO SUGGESTED ALLOCATIONS

Fund	Aggressive	Moderate	Conservative
Schwab U.S. Large Cap	11%	6%	4%
Vanguard Value	11%	7%	5%
Schwab U.S. Small Cap	11%	6%	4%
Vanguard Small-Cap Value	12%	7%	5%
Vanguard REIT Index	5%	3%	2%
Schwab International Equity	9%	5%	3%
iShares MSCI EAFE Value Index	9%	6%	4%
Vanguard FTSE All-Wld ex-U.S. Small-Cap Index	9%	5%	3%
Wisdom Tree International Small-Cap Div	9%	6%	4%
Schwab Emerging Markets Equity	9%	6%	4%
Vanguard Global ex-U.S. Real Estate	5%	3%	2%
iShares Barclays 3-7-Year Treasury Bond	0%	20%	30%
iShares Barclays 1-3-Year Treasury Bond	0%	12%	18%
iShares Barclays TIPS Bond	0%	8%	12%

Some investors don't have enough money to meet the fund minimums imposed by mutual fund families. Many other investors have IRAs and other accounts with which they can "fill in the blanks" of asset classes that are missing in their retirement plans at work.

These investors can use the ETFs listed here, available through brokerage accounts, to build good equity portfolios.

Vanguard

VANGUARD MONTHLY INCOME PORTFOLIO

Fund	Allocation
Vanguard Short-Term Investment Grade	25%
Vanguard Intermediate-Term Investment Grade	25%
Vanguard GNMA	25%
Vanguard High-Yield Corporate	25%

These four funds, selected for Vanguard investors seeking monthly income, are not meant to emulate any part of the Ultimate Buy-and-Hold Strategy. They are my picks for the best low-cost funds to generate current income.

This portfolio is not meant to dampen the volatility of an equity portfolio, so don't use it for that. Nor is it meant to produce capital gains or avoid capital losses, so don't use it for that either. I chose these funds to produce income for your living expenses or other obligations. Use them for that.

APPENDIX F
Getting the Most from the 50 Largest Employer Retirement Plans

I have studied the employee retirement plans for the U.S. government and the largest corporate employers. In the following pages you will find my specific recommendations for the best investment choices in the 50 largest plans in the country.

I believe most participants in these plans will find what they need in the aggressive, moderate, and conservative allocations suggested. In order to understand the following suggestions, you should know a couple of things.

- First, we obtained the data underlying our recommendations from BrightScope Inc.'s proprietary retirement plan database, which is comprised of public data aggregated from the U.S. Department of Labor, including Form 5500s and the associated audit reports. We believe the information accurately reflects the latest public data available at the time we compiled these recommendations.

- Second, the recommendations are based on my choices of asset classes as detailed in Appendix C, "The Ultimate Buy-and-Hold Strategy." None of the following recommendations is perfect because they are limited by the options that each plan has chosen to make available to employees.

This second point is worth discussing because it demonstrates the problem facing workers who want to make the most of their savings. I believe that investors who are either saving for retirement or are already retired should have access to 14 asset classes that I have described in Appendix C, "The Ultimate Buy-and-Hold Strategy."

Not even one of the 50 retirement plans described here offers their employees all 14 of those asset classes. While I don't expect everybody to agree with my choices, each recommendation is there for a specific, legitimate reason. None is frivolous.

Somehow, the teachings of University Street have not trickled down to the people who choose options for retirement plans. The trustees of retirement plans may not have a legal fiduciary duty to the plan participants. But in my view they have an important moral and social duty, as employers cut back traditional pensions, to let plan participants do the best possible job of helping themselves.

Two companies on this list, Fidelity Investments and Shell, have the best plans here. Each of those plans offers 13 of my 14 recommended asset classes, everything except international small-cap value. I admit there are not many mutual funds in that asset class, but low-cost exchange-traded funds (ETFs) are readily available that could be added to any plan.

British Petroleum and General Motors each offer 11 of my favored asset classes, and five other plans offer 10 each, showing that they care about their employees.

At the other end of the spectrum, Exxon Mobil's plan offers only four choices. Another six plans, including that of the U.S. government, offer only five each. While Fidelity does a commendable job of offering its 401(k) participants a range of asset classes from which to choose, I find it startling that other companies in the financial industry don't. The JPMorgan Chase plan includes only six of my recommended asset classes. Prudential Financial offers only seven, Wells Fargo only eight.

Retirement Plan Recommendations

To supplement the recommendations you will find here, I believe investors should use individual retirement accounts (IRAs) to fill in the missing asset classes. This may eliminate or reduce the tax deduction of a traditional 401(k), and it will make rebalancing less convenient. But until employers do a better job of giving their workers what they need, this is the best solution that I know.

Here are my recommendations.

3M COMPANY RETIREMENT PLAN SUGGESTED ALLOCATIONS

Fund	Aggressive	Moderate	Conservative
SSgA S&P 500 Flagship	15%	9%	6%
SSgA Russell 1000 Value Index	20%	12%	8%
SSgA Russell 2000 Index	30%	18%	12%
SSgA Daily EAFE Index Fund	35%	21%	14%
Galliard Stable Value Fund	0%	40%	60%

ABBOTT LABORATORIES RETIREMENT PLAN SUGGESTED ALLOCATIONS

Fund	Aggressive	Moderate	Conservative
Vanguard Instl Ttl Stk Mkt Index	15%	9%	6%
American Funds Washington Mutual R5	15%	9%	6%
Vanguard Extended Market Idx Instl	15%	9%	6%
BlackRock Mid-Cap Value Equity Instl	15%	9%	6%
BlackRock International Opp Instl	20%	12%	8%
American Funds EuroPacific Gr R5	20%	12%	8%
PIMCO Total Return Instl	0%	28%	42%
BNY Mellon Short-Term Investment Fund	0%	12%	18%

AMERICAN AIRLINES RETIREMENT PLAN SUGGESTED ALLOCATIONS

Fund	Aggressive	Moderate	Conservative
American Beacon S&P 500 Idx Instl	12%	7%	5%
Dodge & Cox Stock	13%	8%	5%
American Beacon Small-Cap Idx Inst	12%	7%	5%
American Beacon Small-Cap Val AMR	13%	8%	5%
American Beacon Intl Equity Index Inst	20%	12%	8%
American Beacon Intl Equity AMR	21%	12%	8%
American Beacon Emerging Mkts AMR	0%	6%	4%
Fidelity US Bond Index	0%	20%	30%
American Beacon Short-Term Bond Instl	0%	12%	18%
American Beacon Treas Infl Prot Sec I	0%	8%	12%

AT&T RETIREMENT PLAN SUGGESTED ALLOCATIONS

Fund	Aggressive	Moderate	Conservative
BlackRock US Equity Market Index	25%	15%	10%
BlackRock Extended Equity Market Index	25%	15%	10%
BlackRock EAFE Equity Index Fund	25%	15%	10%
BlackRock International Stock	25%	15%	10%
BlackRock Intermediate Government Index	0%	28%	42%
AT&T Interest Income Fund	0%	12%	18%

BANK OF AMERICA RETIREMENT PLAN SUGGESTED ALLOCATIONS

Fund	Aggressive	Moderate	Conservative
Vanguard Instl Ttl Stk Mkt Idx Instl	10%	6%	4%
Dodge & Cox Stock	10%	6%	4%
Columbia Small Cap Index Z	20%	12%	8%
Fidelity Real Estate Investment	10%	6%	4%
Columbia Multi-Advisor Intl Equity Z	25%	15%	10%
Fidelity Diversified International	25%	15%	10%
Western Asset Core Bond I	0%	20%	30%
Bank of America Stable Value Fund	0%	12%	18%
Vanguard Inflation-Protected Secs Instl	0%	8%	12%

BOEING RETIREMENT PLAN SUGGESTED ALLOCATIONS

Fund	Aggressive	Moderate	Conservative
SSgA S&P 500 Flagship	20%	12%	8%
Northern Trust Russell 2000 Equity Index	20%	12%	8%
BlackRock US Real Estate Index	10%	6%	4%
SSgA Daily EAFE Index Fund	40%	24%	16%
iShares MSCI Emerging Market Index	10%	6%	4%
SSgA Passive Bond Market Index	0%	20%	30%
SSgA Stable Value	0%	12%	18%
BlackRock US TIPS	0%	8%	12%

BRITISH PETROLEUM RETIREMENT PLAN SUGGESTED ALLOCATIONS

Fund	Aggressive	Moderate	Conservative
SSgA S&P 500 Index	10%	6%	4%
Vanguard Windsor Adm	10%	6%	4%
SSgA Russell 2000 Index	10%	6%	4%
BlackRock Russell 2000 Value Index	10%	6%	4%
Fidelity Real Estate Investment	10%	6%	4%
SSgA International Stock Index	20%	12%	8%
Templeton Foreign Adv	20%	12%	8%
Fidelity Emerging Markets K	10%	6%	4%
USAA GNMA	0%	20%	30%
SSgA Short Term Investment Fund	0%	12%	18%
SSgA Treasury Inflation-Protected Securities	0%	8%	12%

CARGILL RETIREMENT PLAN SUGGESTED ALLOCATIONS

Fund	Aggressive	Moderate	Conservative
Vanguard 500 Index Admiral	17%	10%	7%
Vanguard Windsor II Adm	18%	11%	7%
T. Rowe Price Small-Cap Stock	30%	18%	12%
Vanguard Total Intl Stock Index Inv	35%	21%	14%
PIMCO Total Return Instl	0%	28%	42%
SSgA Short Term Investment Fund	0%	12%	18%

CHEVRON RETIREMENT PLAN SUGGESTED ALLOCATIONS

Fund	Aggressive	Moderate	Conservative
Vanguard Institutional Index Instl Pl	15%	9%	6%
Vanguard Windsor II Adm	15%	9%	6%
Neuberger Berman Genesis Instl	15%	9%	6%
Artisan Small Cap Value Investor	15%	9%	6%
American Funds EuroPacific Gr R6	25%	9%	6%
Vanguard Developed Markets Index Inv	0%	15%	10%
Vanguard GNMA Adm	0%	40%	60%

CISCO RETIREMENT PLAN SUGGESTED ALLOCATIONS

Fund	Aggressive	Moderate	Conservative
BlackRock US Equity Market Index	15%	9%	6%
Invesco Large-Cap Rel Val Y	15%	9%	6%
Wells Fargo Advantage Small Cp Val Instl	30%	18%	12%
Harbor International Instl	20%	12%	8%
Fidelity International Discovery	20%	12%	8%
BlackRock US Debt Index	0%	40%	60%

CITIGROUP RETIREMENT PLAN SUGGESTED ALLOCATIONS

Fund	Aggressive	Moderate	Conservative
SPDR S&P 500	20%	12%	8%
SSgA Russell 2000 Index	20%	12%	8%
SSgA REIT Index	10%	6%	4%
SSgA MSCI EAFE Index	20%	12%	8%
DFA Intl Core Equity I	20%	12%	8%
SSgA MSCI Emerging Market Free	10%	6%	4%
SSgA BlackRock Aggregate Bond Index	0%	20%	30%
Citifunds Institutional US Treasury Reserves	0%	12%	18%
SSgA BlackRock US TIPS Fund	0%	8%	12%

CONOCO PHILIPS RETIREMENT PLAN SUGGESTED ALLOCATIONS

Fund	Aggressive	Moderate	Conservative
Vanguard 500 Index Signal	12%	7%	5%
Vanguard Value Index Signal	13%	8%	5%
Vanguard Small-Cap Growth Index Instl	7%	4%	3%
Vanguard Small-Cap Value Index Instl	18%	11%	7%
Vanguard Total Intl Stock Index Inv	25%	15%	10%
Vanguard International Value Inv	25%	15%	10%
Vanguard Total Bond Market Index Signal	0%	20%	30%
SSgA Stable Value Fund	0%	12%	18%
Vanguard Inflation-Protected Secs Instl	0%	8%	12%

CVS CAREMARK RETIREMENT PLAN SUGGESTED ALLOCATIONS

Fund	Aggressive	Moderate	Conservative
Vanguard Institutional Index Instl Pl	25%	15%	10%
Vanguard Small-Cap Index Instl	12%	7%	5%
CVS Small-Cap Value	13%	8%	5%
Templeton Instl Foreign Eq Ser Primary	25%	15%	10%
Vanguard Developed Markets Index Instl	25%	15%	10%
PIMCO Total Return Instl	0%	28%	42%
SSgA Stable Fixed Income	0%	12%	18%

DOW CHEMICAL COMPANY RETIREMENT PLAN SUGGESTED ALLOCATIONS

Fund	Aggressive	Moderate	Conservative
Vanguard Index Equity Fund	10%	6%	4%
Vanguard Windsor II Adm	10%	6%	4%
BlackRock Russell 2000 Index	20%	12%	8%
American Century Real Estate Instl	10%	6%	4%
Vanguard Developed Markets Index Instl	20%	12%	8%
Capital Guardian International Small Cap	20%	12%	8%
Fidelity Emerging Markets	10%	6%	4%
Vanguard Total Bond Market Index Inst	0%	32%	48%
PIMCO Real Return Instl	0%	8%	12%

DUPONT RETIREMENT PLAN SUGGESTED ALLOCATIONS

Fund	Aggressive	Moderate	Conservative
Northern Trust S&P 500 Index	20%	12%	8%
Northern Trust Russell 2000 Equity Index	20%	12%	8%
Natixis AEW Real Estate Y	10%	6%	4%
Northern Trust EAFE Index	12%	7%	5%
AllianceBern Intl Val I	13%	8%	5%
DFA Intl Small-Cap Value I	25%	15%	10%
Northern Trust Aggregate Bond Index	0%	20%	30%
Northern Trust Collective Government Short-Term Investment	0%	12%	18%
Northern Trust TIPS	0%	8%	12%

EXXON MOBIL RETIREMENT PLAN SUGGESTED ALLOCATIONS

Fund	Aggressive	Moderate	Conservative
Northern Trust S&P 500 Index	30%	18%	12%
Northern Trust Small Company Index	40%	24%	16%
Northern Trust EAFE Index	30%	18%	12%
Northern Trust Aggregate Bond Index	0%	40%	60%

FEDEX RETIREMENT PLAN SUGGESTED ALLOCATIONS

Fund	Aggressive	Moderate	Conservative
Vanguard 500 Index Signal	12%	7%	5%
Vanguard Windsor Adm	13%	8%	5%
Vanguard Small-Cap Index Inv	25%	15%	10%
Vanguard Total Intl Stock Index Inv	25%	15%	10%
Vanguard International Value Inv	25%	15%	10%
Vanguard Total Bond Market Index Inst	0%	32%	48%
Vanguard Inflation-Protected Secs Inv	0%	8%	12%

FIDELITY RETIREMENT PLAN SUGGESTED ALLOCATIONS

Fund	Aggressive	Moderate	Conservative
Fidelity Spartan 500 Index Inv	11%	6%	4%
Fidelity Large-Cap Value Enhanced Index	11%	7%	5%
Fidelity Small-Cap Enhanced Index	11%	7%	4%
Fidelity Small-Cap Value	12%	7%	5%
Fidelity Real Estate Investment	5%	3%	2%
Fidelity Spartan International Index Inv	9%	6%	3%
Fidelity International Value	18%	10%	7%
Fidelity International Small-Cap Opp	9%	5%	4%
Fidelity Emerging Markets	9%	6%	4%
Fidelity International Real Estate	5%	3%	2%
Fidelity Intermediate Government Inc	0%	20%	30%
Fidelity Spartan S/T Tr Bd Index Inv	0%	12%	18%
Fidelity Inflation-Protected Bond	0%	8%	12%

FORD RETIREMENT PLAN SUGGESTED ALLOCATIONS

Fund	Aggressive	Moderate	Conservative
Vanguard Institutional Index Instl Pl	10%	6%	4%
Fidelity Equity-Income	10%	6%	4%
Comerica Small-Cap Index Fund	20%	12%	8%
Fidelity Real Estate Investment	10%	6%	4%
BlackRock EAFE Equity Index Fund	25%	15%	10%
T. Rowe Price International Discovery	25%	15%	10%
BlackRock US Debt Index	0%	20%	30%
Comerica ShortTerm Fund	0%	12%	18%
PIMCO Real Return Instl	0%	8%	12%

GE RETIREMENT PLAN SUGGESTED ALLOCATIONS

Fund	Aggressive	Moderate	Conservative
US Large-Cap Equity Fund	25%	15%	10%
US Small-Cap Equity Index Fund	25%	15%	10%
GE Instl International Equity Inv	25%	15%	10%
Non US Equity Index Fund	25%	15%	10%
TIPS Index Fund MISC	0%	20%	30%
US Aggregate Bond Index Fund	0%	20%	30%

GENERAL MOTORS RETIREMENT PLAN SUGGESTED ALLOCATIONS

Fund	Aggressive	Moderate	Conservative
SSgA S&P 500 Flagship	11%	6%	4%
Bernstein Diversified Value	12%	7%	5%
SSgA Russell Small-Cap Completeness Index	22%	14%	9%
SSgA REIT Index	5%	3%	2%
Fidelity Diversified International	10%	6%	4%
SSgA Daily EAFE Index Fund	25%	15%	10%
SSgA Emerging Markets	10%	6%	4%
Invesco Global Real Estate A	5%	3%	2%
PIMCO Total Return	0%	20%	30%
SSgA Short-Term Investment Fund	0%	12%	18%
PIMCO Real Return	0%	8%	12%

GLAXOSMITHKLINE RETIREMENT PLAN SUGGESTED ALLOCATIONS

Fund	Aggressive	Moderate	Conservative
SSgA S&P 500 Flagship	12%	7%	5%
Vanguard Windsor II Adm	13%	8%	5%
SSgA Russell 2000 Index	25%	15%	10%
SSgA Daily EAFE Index Fund	25%	15%	10%
Templeton Foreign Adv	25%	15%	10%
SSgA Passive Bond Market Index	0%	28%	42%
SSgA Short-Term Investment Fund	0%	12%	18%

GOLDMAN SACHS GROUP RETIREMENT PLAN SUGGESTED ALLOCATIONS

Fund	Aggressive	Moderate	Conservative
Goldman Sachs Structured US Equity I	10%	6%	4%
BlackRock Equity Value	15%	9%	6%
SSgA Russell 2000 Index	25%	15%	10%
Goldman Sachs Real Estate Instl	10%	6%	4%
GMO Intl Intrinsic Value IV	30%	18%	12%
SSgA Emerging Markets	10%	6%	4%
Western Asset Core Plus Bond IS	0%	20%	30%
Goldman Sachs Short Dur Govt Instl	0%	12%	18%
SSgA Treasury Inflation-Protected Sec Index	0%	8%	12%

HCA RETIREMENT PLAN SUGGESTED ALLOCATIONS

Fund	Aggressive	Moderate	Conservative
HCA S&P 500 Index Fund	17%	10%	7%
Large-Company Value Fund	18%	11%	7%
Small-Company Growth Fund	12%	7%	5%
Small-Company Value Fund	23%	14%	9%
HCA International Equity Fund	30%	18%	12%
HCA Fixed Income Fund	0%	28%	42%
Northern Trust Collective Short Term Investment	0%	12%	18%

HEWLETT-PACKARD RETIREMENT PLAN SUGGESTED ALLOCATIONS

Fund	Aggressive	Moderate	Conservative
SPDR S&P 500	12%	7%	5%
Dodge & Cox Stock	13%	8%	5%
Vanguard Extended Market Idx Instl	25%	15%	10%
SSgA Daily EAFE Index Fund	10%	6%	4%
Dodge & Cox International Stock	10%	6%	4%
MFS International New Discovery I	20%	12%	8%
American Funds New World R5	10%	6%	4%
SSgA Passive Bond Market Index	0%	20%	30%
PIMCO Short Term	0%	12%	18%
PIMCO Real Return Instl	0%	8%	12%

HONEYWELL RETIREMENT PLAN SUGGESTED ALLOCATIONS

Fund	Aggressive	Moderate	Conservative
SSgA S&P 500 Flagship	25%	15%	10%
Vanguard Windsor II Adm	25%	15%	10%
SSgA Daily EAFE Index Fund	30%	18%	12%
BlackRock Emerging Markets Equity	10%	6%	4%
Northern Trust Global Real Estate	10%	6%	4%
BlackRock US Debt Index	0%	28%	42%
SSgA Government Short Term Investment Fund	0%	12%	18%

IBM RETIREMENT PLAN SUGGESTED ALLOCATIONS

Fund	Aggressive	Moderate	Conservative
Vanguard Large-Cap Index	15%	9%	6%
Vanguard Large-Cap Value Index	15%	9%	6%
IBM Small/Mid-Cap Stock	15%	9%	6%
Vanguard Small-Cap Value Index	15%	9%	6%
IBM Real Estate Investment Trust	5%	3%	2%
IBM Total International Stock Market	30%	18%	12%
IBM International Real Estate	5%	3%	2%
IBM Inflation Protected Bond	0%	20%	30%
IBM Total Bond Market	0%	20%	30%

JOHNSON & JOHNSON RETIREMENT PLAN SUGGESTED ALLOCATIONS

Fund	Aggressive	Moderate	Conservative
Johnson & Johnson JJ5D Russell 3000	30%	18%	12%
Johnson & Johnson JJ8K Small Cap Composite	40%	24%	16%
Johnson & Johnson JJ3C Intl Equity Core	30%	18%	12%
Johnson & Johnson JJ2C Intermediate Bond	0%	28%	42%
Johnson & Johnson JJ5H Short-Term Investments	0%	12%	18%

JPMORGAN CHASE & CO. RETIREMENT PLAN SUGGESTED ALLOCATIONS

Fund	Aggressive	Moderate	Conservative
JPMorgan US Equity	17%	10%	7%
BlackRock Russell 1000 Value Index	18%	11%	7%
JPMorgan Small-Cap Core	25%	15%	10%
iShares MSCI EAFE Index	40%	24%	16%
JPMorgan Core Bond	0%	28%	42%
SSgA Guaranteed Investment Contract	0%	12%	18%

LIBERTY MUTUAL GROUP RETIREMENT PLAN SUGGESTED ALLOCATIONS

Fund	Aggressive	Moderate	Conservative
BlackRock Equity Index	25%	15%	10%
SSgA Russell 2000 Index	25%	15%	10%
BlackRock EAFE Equity Index Fund	40%	24%	16%
Capital Guardian Emerging Markets Equity	10%	6%	4%
Wellington Inflation Protected Core Bond	0%	16%	24%
Northern Trust Short Term	0%	24%	36%

LOCKHEED MARTIN RETIREMENT PLAN SUGGESTED ALLOCATIONS

Fund	Aggressive	Moderate	Conservative
Lockheed Martin S&P 500 Index	12%	7%	5%
Lockheed Martin Value Equity Fund	13%	7%	5%
Lockheed Martin Small/Mid-Cap Index	26%	16%	10%
Lockheed Martin MSCI EAFE Index	30%	18%	12%

LOCKHEED MARTIN RETIREMENT PLAN SUGGESTED ALLOCATIONS (CONTINUED)

Fund	Aggressive	Moderate	Conservative
Lockheed Martin Global Real Estate Fund	10%	6%	4%
Lockheed Martin Emerging Markets Index	9%	6%	4%
Lockheed Martin Broad Market Bond Index	0%	20%	30%
Lockheed Martin Treas Infl-Protected Secs	0%	8%	12%
Lockheed Martin Govt ST Investment Fund	0%	12%	18%

MICROSOFT RETIREMENT PLAN SUGGESTED ALLOCATIONS

Fund	Aggressive	Moderate	Conservative
Vanguard Institutional Index Instl	12%	7%	5%
Vanguard Value Index Instl	13%	8%	5%
Russell US Small & Mid-Cap Y	25%	15%	10%
Russell International Value	33%	20%	13%
Russell International Growth	17%	10%	7%
PIMCO Total Return Instl	0%	28%	42%
Vanguard Short-Term Bond Index Adm	0%	12%	18%

MORGAN STANLEY RETIREMENT PLAN SUGGESTED ALLOCATIONS

Fund	Aggressive	Moderate	Conservative
Invesco Van Kampen Growth and Income Y	15%	9%	6%
Morgan Stanley Inst Opportunity I	5%	3%	2%
Royce Special Equity Instl	20%	12%	8%
Morgan Stanley Inst US Real Estate I	10%	6%	4%
BlackRock MSCI ACWI ex-US Index	20%	12%	8%
Pyramis Select International Small Cap	20%	12%	8%
Morgan Stanley Inst Emerging Mkts I	10%	6%	4%
BlackRock US Debt Index	0%	20%	30%
Bank of America GIC	0%	12%	18%
PIMCO Real Return Instl	0%	8%	12%

MOTOROLA RETIREMENT PLAN SUGGESTED ALLOCATIONS

Fund	Aggressive	Moderate	Conservative
Northern Trust S&P 500 Index Lending	30%	18%	12%
Northern Trust Russell 2000 Equity Index Lending	30%	18%	12%
Northern Trust EAFE Index	40%	24%	16%
Northern Trust Aggregate Bond Index	0%	28%	42%
Northern Trust Collective Short Term Investment	0%	12%	18%

NORTHROP GRUMMAN RETIREMENT PLAN SUGGESTED ALLOCATIONS

Fund	Aggressive	Moderate	Conservative
Northrop Grumman DC MT Equity Index Fund	30%	18%	12%
Northrop Grumman DC MT Small-Cap Fund	30%	18%	12%
Northrop Grumman DC MT International Equity Fund	30%	18%	12%
Northrop Grumman DC MT Emerging Markets Fund	10%	6%	4%
Northrop Grumman DC MT Fixed Income Fund	0%	28%	42%
SSgA Short-Term Investment Fund	0%	12%	18%

PFIZER RETIREMENT PLAN SUGGESTED ALLOCATIONS

Fund	Aggressive	Moderate	Conservative
Northern Trust S&P 500 Index Lending	17%	10%	7%
Eaton Vance Large-Cap Value I	18%	11%	7%
T. Rowe Price Small-Cap Stock	30%	18%	12%
Dodge & Cox International Stock	35%	21%	14%
BlackRock US Debt Index	0%	20%	30%
Northern Trust Collective ST Investment	0%	12%	18%
BlackRock US TIPS	0%	8%	12%

PRUDENTIAL FINANCIAL RETIREMENT PLAN SUGGESTED ALLOCATIONS

Fund	Aggressive	Moderate	Conservative
Prudential Stock Index I	15%	9%	5%
Prudential Large Value/LSV Asset Management	15%	9%	6%
Prudential Small Company Stock	25%	15%	10%
Prudential International Equity Z	35%	21%	14%
Prudential Global Real Estate	10%	6%	4%
Fidelity Advisor Government Income I	0%	28%	42%
PESP Fixed Rate Fund	0%	12%	18%

RAYTHEON RETIREMENT PLAN SUGGESTED ALLOCATIONS

Fund	Aggressive	Moderate	Conservative
Vanguard Morgan Growth Adm	6%	4%	3%
Vanguard Windsor Adm	19%	11%	7%
T. Rowe Price Small-Cap Stock	12%	7%	5%
American Century Small-Cap Value Instl	13%	8%	5%
BlackRock EAFE Equity Index Fund	12%	7%	5%
Dodge & Cox International Stock	13%	8%	5%
Oppenheimer International Small-Co Y	6%	4%	3%
First Eagle Overseas I	19%	11%	7%
Fidelity Spartan Interm Tr Bond Idx Inv	0%	28%	42%
Fidelity Short-Term Investment Fund	0%	12%	18%

SAIC RETIREMENT PLAN SUGGESTED ALLOCATIONS

Fund	Aggressive	Moderate	Conservative
Vanguard 500 Index Admiral	12%	7%	5%
Dodge & Cox Stock	13%	8%	5%
Vanguard Small-Cap Index Instl	25%	15%	10%
Vanguard Developed Markets Index Instl	20%	12%	8%
Templeton Foreign Adv	20%	12%	8%
Morgan Stanley Inst Emerging Markets I	10%	6%	4%
Vanguard Total Bond Market Index Inst	0%	28%	42%
Vanguard Short-Term Bond Index Adm	0%	12%	18%

SHELL RETIREMENT PLAN SUGGESTED ALLOCATIONS

Fund	Aggressive	Moderate	Conservative
Fidelity Spartan 500 Index Inv	11%	6%	4%
BlackRock Russell 1000 Value Index	11%	7%	5%
Fidelity Small-Cap Enhanced Index	11%	7%	4%
Fidelity Small-Cap Value	12%	7%	5%
Fidelity Real Estate Investment	5%	3%	2%
Fidelity Spartan International Index	9%	5%	3%
Fidelity International Value	9%	5%	4%
Fidelity International Small Cap	18%	11%	7%
Fidelity Emerging Markets	9%	6%	4%
Fidelity International Real Estate	5%	3%	2%
Fidelity Intermediate Government	0%	20%	30%
Fidelity S/T Tr Bond Index	0%	12%	18%
Fidelity Inflation Protected Bond	0%	8%	12%

SIEMENS RETIREMENT PLAN SUGGESTED ALLOCATIONS

Fund	Aggressive	Moderate	Conservative
Equity Index Trust	25%	15%	10%
SSgA Russell 2000 Index	25%	15%	10%
BlackRock EAFE Equity Index Fund	40%	22%	14%
Emerging Market Equity Fund MISC	10%	8%	6%
SSgA Stable Value Fund	0%	40%	60%

SUPERVALU RETIREMENT PLAN SUGGESTED ALLOCATIONS

Fund	Aggressive	Moderate	Conservative
BlackRock Russell 1000 Index	25%	15%	10%
BlackRock Russell 2000 Index	15%	9%	6%
iShares Russell 2000 Value Index	20%	12%	8%
BlackRock MSCI ACWI ex-US Index	30%	18%	12%
BlackRock Global Emerging Markets	10%	6%	4%
BlackRock US Debt Index	0%	20%	30%
SSgA Short-Term Investment Fund	0%	12%	18%
BlackRock US TIPS	0%	8%	12%

TARGET RETIREMENT PLAN SUGGESTED ALLOCATIONS

Fund	Aggressive	Moderate	Conservative
BlackRock S&P 500 Index Fund	25%	15%	10%
SSgA Russell 2000 Index	25%	15%	10%
BlackRock US Real Estate Index Fund	10%	6%	4%
SSgA Daily EAFE Index Fund	30%	18%	12%
SSgA Emerging Markets	10%	6%	4%
Target Stable Value Fund	0%	24%	36%
SSgA Treasury Inflation-Protected Sec Index	0%	16%	24%

UNITED TECHNOLOGIES RETIREMENT PLAN SUGGESTED ALLOCATIONS

Fund	Aggressive	Moderate	Conservative
SSgA S&P 500 Index	12%	7%	5%
SSgA Russell 1000 Value Index	13%	8%	5%
SSgA Small-Cap Index	12%	7%	5%
Target Small-Capitalization Value T	13%	8%	5%
SSgA International Stock	20%	12%	8%
Templeton Foreign Adv	20%	12%	8%
Templeton Emerging Markets Small Ca A	10%	6%	4%
Synthetic Investment Contracts	0%	40%	60%

UPS RETIREMENT PLAN SUGGESTED ALLOCATIONS

Fund	Aggressive	Moderate	Conservative
Prudential S&P 500 Flagship	25%	15%	10%
Prudential Russell 2000 Index	25%	15%	10%
Prudential REIT Index	10%	6%	4%
Prudential International Index	40%	24%	16%
Prudential Passive Bond Market Index	0%	28%	42%
Prudential Govt Short-Term Inv Fund	0%	12%	18%

U.S. GOVERNMENT RETIREMENT PLAN SUGGESTED ALLOCATIONS

Fund	Aggressive	Moderate	Conservative
C-Fund	30%	18%	12%
S-Fund	40%	24%	16%
I-Fund	30%	18%	12%
F-Fund	0%	28%	42%
G-Fund	0%	12%	18%

VERIZON RETIREMENT PLAN SUGGESTED ALLOCATIONS

Fund	Aggressive	Moderate	Conservative
Clipper	10%	6%	4%
GAMCO Large Cap Value	10%	6%	4%
DFA US Micro Cap I	20%	12%	8%
Pyramis REIT	10%	6%	4%
Fidelity Diversified International	20%	12%	8%
Pyramis Select International Small Cap	20%	12%	8%
DFA Emerging Markets Value I	10%	6%	4%
Fidelity US Bond Index	0%	20%	30%
Fidelity Stable Value Fund	0%	12%	18%
PIMCO Real Return Instl	0%	8%	12%

WALGREENS RETIREMENT PLAN SUGGESTED ALLOCATIONS

Fund	Aggressive	Moderate	Conservative
SSgA S&P 500 Flagship	30%	18%	12%
SSgA Russell 2000 Index	40%	24%	16%
Northern Trust EAFE Index	30%	18%	12%
SSgA Passive Bond Market Index	0%	28%	42%
Northern Trust Collective Short Term Investment	0%	12%	18%

WALMART RETIREMENT PLAN SUGGESTED ALLOCATIONS

Fund	Aggressive	Moderate	Conservative
BlackRock Russell 1000 Index	25%	15%	10%
BlackRock Russell 2000 Index	12%	7%	5%
Westwood Trust SMID Cap Value Equity	13%	8%	5%
BlackRock MSCI ACWI ex-US Index	15%	9%	6%
Mondrian International Value Equity	15%	9%	6%
Victory International Small Cap Equity Trust	20%	12%	8%
PIMCO Total Return Instl	0%	20%	30%
Barclays Treas Inflation Protected Sec Index	0%	8%	12%
MetLife Stable Value Fund	0%	12%	18%

WELLS FARGO RETIREMENT PLAN SUGGESTED ALLOCATIONS

Fund	Aggressive	Moderate	Conservative
Wells Fargo S&P 500 Index	17%	10%	7%
Wells Fargo Large-Cap Value	18%	10%	7%
Wells Fargo Russell 2000 Index	25%	15%	10%
Wells Fargo International Equity Index	15%	9%	6%
American Funds EuroPacific Growth	15%	10%	6%
Wells Fargo Emerging Markets	10%	6%	4%
Wells Fargo US Aggregate Bond Index	0%	28%	42%
Wells Fargo Stable Return Trust	0%	12%	18%

APPENDIX G
"Lazy Portfolios"

In this appendix I look at a handful of proposed mutual fund portfolios designed for investors who don't want to be bothered with a lot of details. After adjusting the allocation percentages so they have roughly equivalent levels of risk, I show how these portfolios performed in a recent 10-year period that included many challenges for investors.

Simplicity still holds a great allure for most of us. Financial writers and commentators are always looking for simple ways to build good portfolios from the offerings within a single mutual fund family.

The eight "lazy portfolios" included here are made up of Vanguard index funds. Each one was proposed as a one-time-only selection that could be purchased and then forgotten. This made things easy. But it also ruled out some important things. Even if new knowledge or new funds became available after this exercise started, no changes were allowed. In other words, these portfolios were locked into the beliefs of the authors at the time and limited to the tools available then.

These portfolios were collected from various sources by Market Watch.com (http://www.marketwatch.com/) columnist Paul Farrell and described in his 2004 book, *The Lazy Person's Guide to Investing: A Book for Procrastinators, the Financially Challenged, and Everyone Who Worries About Dealing with Their Money.*

Farrell tracks and publishes the results of these portfolios at Market Watch.com.

Lazy Portfolios Adjusted for 60 Percent Equity, 40 Percent Fixed Income

Following are the portfolios and their results, as adjusted by Larry Katz, research director at Merriman Inc., through the end of December 2010. (Because of those adjustments, which I will note right below the following table, the returns quoted here are not the same as those published at MarketWatch.com.)

Portfolio	10-Year Annualized Return*
Yale U's Unconventional (David Swenson)	7.3%
Aronson Family Taxable	7.2%
FundAdvice.com Ultimate Buy-and-Hold	7.2%
Coffeehouse	6.5%
Dr. Bernstein's Smart Money	5.9%
Margaritaville	5.7%
Dr. Bernstein's No-Brainer	5.5%
Second Grader's Starter	5.0%

*Returns computed after standardizing fund allocations to reflect a uniform split of 60 percent stock funds and 40 percent bond funds.

The point of showing all these portfolios is to demonstrate the wide variety of possible ways to use Vanguard stock funds.

The following tables list the funds used in each portfolio. Remember, these include only funds that were available some years ago. The authors of these portfolios might make different recommendations today. (For example, now I would include Vanguard's small-cap international and international real estate funds.)

The original fixed-income allocations of these portfolios range from a low of 10 percent in the Second Grader's Starter to a high of 40 percent in the FundAdvice.com Ultimate Buy-and-Hold, Dr. Bernstein's Smart Money, and Coffeehouse portfolios. As noted, in order to compare apples to apples, we recalculated the suggested allocations (which follow) and the portfolios' performances (which you see above) by standardizing the fixed-income part of each one to 40 percent.

We made another important adjustment that makes our returns different from those reported at MarketWatch.com. In the interests of "total laziness," Farrell assumed that money would be put into these funds initially and then never rebalanced. This is not good financial practice because it allows an investor's risk exposure to drift over time.

Therefore, in calculating the performance results we assumed that the funds in each portfolio were rebalanced once a year in order to return them to the allocations you see in each table below. Each portfolio's bond funds are listed first, followed by the equity funds.

YALE U'S UNCONVENTIONAL PORTFOLIO

Vanguard Inflation-Protected Securities (VIPSX)	20.0%
Vanguard Long-Term Treasury (VUSTX)	20.0%
Vanguard Total Stock Market (VTSMX)	25.7%
Vanguard REIT Index (VGSIX)	17.1%
Vanguard Developed Markets (VDMIX)	12.9%
Vanguard Emerging Markets Stock (VEIEX)	4.3%

David Swenson is the manager of Yale University's endowment fund, for which he has generated excellent returns over a long period. In both the bond and stock parts of this portfolio, his fund choices involve more risk than I consider prudent.

For example, I am not comfortable with the idea of holding 20 percent of any portfolio in a long-term bond fund. Long-term bonds have higher expected returns than shorter-term ones, but their volatility can be much greater.

On the equity side, Swenson has virtually no exposure to small-cap stocks or value stocks, and his international exposure is much less than I think is ideal. One thing he does have a lot of is real estate investment trusts (REITs). I believe that largely explains why his portfolio, with no small-company funds and no value funds, had the highest 10-year return on the list. In that particular decade, REITs were star performers.

ARONSON FAMILY TAXABLE PORTFOLIO

Vanguard Inflation-Protected Securities (VIPSX)	20.0%
Vanguard Long-Term Treasury (VUSTX)	13.3%
Vanguard High-Yield Corporate (VWEHX)	6.7%
Vanguard 500 Index (VFINX)	12.9%
Vanguard Pacific Stock Index (VPACX)	12.9%
Vanguard Extended Market Index (VEXMX)	8.6%
Vanguard Emerging Markets Stock (VEIEX)	8.6%
Vanguard Small-Cap Growth Index (VISGX)	4.3%
Vanguard Small-Cap Value Index (VISVX)	4.3%
Vanguard European Stock Index (VEURX)	4.3%
Vanguard Total International Stock (VGTSX)	4.3%

Ted Aronson and his AJO Partners manage about $25 billion of institutional assets. He puts his family's taxable money in the portfolio shown here. His portfolio is weak in value stocks and holds less than mine in international stocks.

FUNDADVICE.COM ULTIMATE BUY-AND-HOLD PORTFOLIO

Vanguard Intermediate-Term Treasury (VFITX)	20.0%
Vanguard Short-Term Treasury (VFISX)	12.0%
Vanguard Inflation-Protected Securities (VIPSX)	8.0%
Vanguard International Value (VTRIX)	12.0%
Vanguard Developed Markets (VDMIX)	12.0%
Vanguard 500 Index (VFINX)	6.0%
Vanguard Small-Cap Index (NAESX)	6.0%
Vanguard Small-Cap Value Index (VISVX)	6.0%
Vanguard Value Index (VIVAX)	6.0%
Vanguard Emerging Markets Stock (VEIEX)	6.0%
Vanguard REIT Index (VGSIX)	6.0%

I, along with my company's research department, helped create this portfolio. Even though Vanguard has funds available now that didn't exist when we put this together, I still think these are fine choices.

COFFEEHOUSE PORTFOLIO

Vanguard Total Bond Market Index (VBMFX)	40.0%
Vanguard Small-Cap Index (NAESX)	10.0%
Vanguard Small-Cap Value Index (VISVX)	10.0%
Vanguard REIT Index (VGSIX)	10.0%
Vanguard Total International Stock (VGTSX)	10.0%
Vanguard 500 Index (VFINX)	10.0%
Vanguard Value Index (VIVAX)	10.0%

Bill Schultheis is an investment advisor and author of *The Coffeehouse Investor.* He may believe that many investors are busy sipping their lattes and don't want to be bothered by fussing over percentage allocations. So in the tug-of-war between simple and sophisticated, he made "simple" the big winner, grabbing the total bond market in one fund and dividing the equity side of his Coffeehouse portfolio equally six ways. He does a good job of picking up value and REITs exposure, but for my taste he is far too heavily invested in U.S. stocks.

DR. BERNSTEIN'S SMART MONEY PORTFOLIO

Vanguard Short-Term Investment Grade (VFSTX)	40.0%
Vanguard Total Stock Market (VTSMX)	15.0%
Vanguard Value Index (VIVAX)	10.0%
Vanguard Small-Cap Value Index (VISVX)	10.0%
Vanguard Small-Cap Index (NAESX)	5.0%
Vanguard REIT Index (VGSIX)	5.0%
Vanguard European Stock Index (VEURX)	5.0%
Vanguard Emerging Markets Stock (VEIEX)	5.0%
Vanguard Pacific Stock Index (VPACX)	5.0%

Dr. William Bernstein is a physician and a financial advisor to high-net-worth individuals. The biggest difference between his Smart Money portfolio and my own is that he allocates only half as much to international stocks.

MARGARITAVILLE PORTFOLIO

Vanguard Inflation-Protected Securities (VIPSX)	40.0%
Vanguard Total Stock Market (VTSMX)	30.0%
Vanguard Total International Stock (VGTSX)	30.0%

The Margaritaville portfolio of newspaper columnist Scott Burns is very easy to mix. One part inflation-protected securities, one part U.S. stocks, and one part international stocks. If you believe the titles of his two equity funds, it looks like you get the whole enchilada to wash down with your margarita. However, the word *total* in the titles of those two stock funds is deceptive.

Yes, those funds include some value stocks and some small-company stocks. But no, they don't provide a balance. Those funds are constructed to reflect the capitalization of the market as a whole, giving much more weight to huge companies like General Electric and Citicorp than to small ones like Informatica Corp. and Williams-Sonoma, two of the largest companies in Vanguard's U.S. small-cap index fund.

The Vanguard Total Stock Market Fund, for example, has only 9 percent of its portfolio in small-company stocks, far from the 50 percent that I believe is the right allocation.

DR. BERNSTEIN'S NO BRAINER PORTFOLIO

Vanguard Total Bond Market Index (VBMFX)	40.0%
Vanguard Small-Cap Index (NAESX)	20.0%
Vanguard European Stock Index (VEURX)	20.0%
Vanguard 500 Index (VFINX)	20.0%

This portfolio has no value fund at all and puts two-thirds of its equity exposure in the U.S. stock market. On the international side, the portfolio has no way to participate in Asia and emerging markets.

SECOND GRADER'S STARTER PORTFOLIO

Vanguard Total Bond Market Index (VBMFX)	40.0%
Vanguard Total Stock Market (VTSMX)	40.0%
Vanguard Total International Stock (VGTSX)	20.0%

Eight-year-old Kevin devised this portfolio, with a little help from his father, Allan Roth, a registered investment advisor and online columnist, in addition to a generous gift from his grandmother. For a very young investor who is just starting out and does not have a lot of money, this is a good beginning. To a second grader, the word *total* has to be very appealing.

I'm grateful to Paul Farrell for writing a book about lazy portfolios and for letting us see the results. Investing doesn't have to be complicated, and sometimes lazy is good. As I said in the Introduction to this book, getting your portfolio allocated just right may require the equivalent of a week's work, plus perhaps two hours a year to keep it in shape. After that, you've got the rest of your life to be lazy.

APPENDIX H
Withdrawing Money when You're Retired

If you are retired or seriously thinking about how to finance your retirement years, study the information in this appendix.

When you reach retirement, four major decisions will determine the bulk of your financial future. This appendix is about two of those decisions.

- How much income do you need or want from your retirement portfolio?
- Do you need a fixed stream of income you can count on, or can you tolerate cash flow that goes up and down depending on the success of your investments?

You may have saved for decades and invested your money carefully. But when the money must start flowing in the opposite direction—from your portfolio to you—you are suddenly faced with a whole new set of challenging choices.

This appendix is built around four tables that my company has found to be very useful when we work with clients.

But before we get to them, let me back up a moment. I mentioned four major financial decisions that will shape your future once you retire. In addition to the two we are examining here, the other two are:

- How will you invest your money?
- How much risk will you take with your investments?

These last two questions are extremely important, and I've discussed each of them in the body of this book and in even more detail in the first three appendixes.

Taking Money from Your Portfolio

How much do you want or need from your portfolio? Should that amount be fixed or variable? Only you can give the final answers to those questions, which involve important variables. Every situation is different, and without knowing your circumstances, I cannot give you the answers that are best for you. I believe you will probably get the best answers with the help of a professional financial advisor. Here I can at least identify some of the most important issues and give you a head start in thinking about them.

Here's an important note: Because of investors' concerns about future inflation, the distributions shown in two of the four tables have been adjusted for actual inflation during the years in this study.

This appendix describes two possible withdrawal rates: 4 percent, which I regard as conservative, and 6 percent, which may be too aggressive for many investors. It's easy to split the difference and choose a more moderate 5 percent. But for our purposes, I'm showing only 4 percent and 6 percent.

The tables show returns of globally diversified portfolios built with Dimensional Fund Advisors mutual funds. The returns assume transaction costs and management fees of 1 percent annually.

Fixed or Variable Withdrawals

A major decision you make when you retire is whether to choose a fixed withdrawal plan or a flexible one. Let's start with the fixed plan.

For this discussion, I'll assume you retire with a $1 million portfolio that includes equity funds that are well diversified as described in the body of this book. I'll assume that you need to supplement your other income (Social Security, pension, rental income, and so forth) by taking out either $40,000 (conservative) or $60,000 (aggressive) in the first year. And I'll assume you will need to adjust that annual withdrawal every year to keep up with inflation.

We'll refer to this plan as a fixed distribution schedule. Although the withdrawal each year will change, you will maintain a fixed amount of spending power each year as determined by changes in the Consumer Price Index. For the historical numbers in our tables, we have used actual inflation, which gives a more realistic picture than simple assumptions based on flat rates of inflation.

Studying the Numbers

The following table shows the results of the aggressive variation of the fixed withdrawal plan beginning in 1970, the earliest year for which I have full data, through 2010.

AGGRESSIVE FIXED DISTRIBUTION SCHEDULE*

	40% Global Equity	50% Global Equity	60% Global Equity	S&P 500 Index W/Divs	Distributions
1970	997,006	980,845	964,684	977,845	60,000
1971	1,076,699	1,079,063	1,080,686	1,045,379	63,396
1972	1,142,313	1,169,174	1,195,276	1,165,860	65,466
1973	1,014,400	1,015,568	1,014,871	937,108	67,696
1974	881,973	854,291	824,901	635,046	73,590
1975	976,462	972,719	964,590	757,927	82,669
1976	1,014,151	1,022,348	1,025,302	829,197	88,404
1977	1,029,301	1,061,356	1,087,693	683,618	92,704
1978	1,050,099	1,114,904	1,174,814	623,139	98,916
1979	1,022,011	1,102,123	1,177,405	610,242	107,836
1980	1,023,065	1,136,202	1,246,501	646,242	122,172
1981	936,163	1,049,953	1,159,269	483,804	137,464
1982	933,954	1,059,003	1,176,803	405,599	149,729
1983	902,575	1,069,630	1,234,580	306,451	155,463

continued

AGGRESSIVE FIXED DISTRIBUTION SCHEDULE* (CONTINUED)

	40% Global Equity	50% Global Equity	60% Global Equity	S&P 500 Index W/Divs	Distributions
1984	815,013	993,388	1,168,528	154,187	161,356
1985	812,878	1,057,152	1,306,459		167,728
1986	771,064	1,087,020	1,422,386		174,099
1987	641,543	997,256	1,386,450		176,011
1988	516,692	936,776	1,412,719		183,816
1989	374,317	870,095	1,443,499		191,939
1990	169,441	645,897	1,175,577		200,859
1991		519,520	1,173,644		213,124
1992		311,403	994,969		219,655
1993		97,792	921,909		226,026
1994			684,066		232,239
1995			510,706		238,451
1996			285,791		244,504
1997			31,667		252,627
1998					256,928
1999					261,069
2000					268,078
2001					277,157
2002					281,458
2003					288,148
2004					293,564
2005					303,121
2006					313,474
2007					321,439
2008					334,557
2009					334,863
2010					343,976

*See text for explanation. Data copyright © 2011 Merriman, Inc.

Here's how to read the table. On the far right side is a column showing the actual distribution every year, which is derived from actual inflation in the previous year. For example, inflation in 1970 was 5.66 percent, and that raised the 1971 distribution to $63,396.

The other columns show the year-end values of the portfolio for three asset allocations: 40 percent equities, 50 percent equities, and 60 percent equities. A fourth column of values shows the results of having the entire portfolio invested in the Standard & Poor's 500 Index.

When you look at these four columns of returns, you will immediately notice the white space at the bottom. That's because those four portfolios ran out of money under these assumptions.

For example, if you had invested exclusively in the Standard & Poor's 500 Index, by the end of 1984 your portfolio would have been worth only $154,187 (down from $1 million to start) and about to go broke paying you what it could of the $167,728 that your plan said you would have needed in 1985. After that, the money was gone.

In the other columns, you will see that you would have done a little better with diversified equities. The 60 percent equity portfolio would have lasted an additional dozen years. But it would have been broke in 1997. The portfolios with 40 percent and 50 percent in equities ran out sooner.

Three things become pretty obvious. First, portfolios that contained more equities, with proper diversification, provided distributions that lasted longer. Second, proper equity diversification was such a big improvement that even a portfolio made up of 60 percent bond funds did better than the S&P 500. Third, none of these portfolios could keep up with the relentless inflation-adjusted withdrawals that we assumed would be necessary.

A Balancing Act

As the previous table shows, risk and return are a balancing act. You can also see the huge effect that inflation can have over time. An annual withdrawal that started out as a "mere" $60,000 in 1970 had more than doubled by 1980—and it grew to about $200,000 by 1990.

Now that you know how to read this table, you won't have trouble seeing a quite different set of results in the next table, which is based on much more conservative distributions starting at $40,000.

CONSERVATIVE FIXED DISTRIBUTION SCHEDULE*

	40% Global Equity	50% Global Equity	60% Global Equity	S&P 500 Index W/Divs	Distributions
1970	1,018,465	1,001,956	985,447	998,650	40,000
1971	1,126,211	1,129,148	1,131,237	1,093,321	42,264
1972	1,223,884	1,253,132	1,281,522	1,248,862	43,644
1973	1,113,490	1,114,564	1,113,579	1,027,193	45,131
1974	998,757	967,185	933,738	719,336	49,060
1975	1,153,486	1,150,484	1,142,577	911,393	55,113
1976	1,251,379	1,263,363	1,269,511	1,055,759	58,936
1977	1,330,859	1,373,901	1,410,715	922,597	61,803
1978	1,430,509	1,518,133	1,601,430	912,969	65,944
1979	1,477,143	1,586,007	1,691,672	996,038	71,891
1980	1,590,925	1,748,298	1,906,637	1,210,988	81,448
1981	1,589,733	1,746,484	1,902,101	1,064,399	91,642
1982	1,775,560	1,944,202	2,107,793	1,171,091	99,819
1983	1,946,377	2,187,918	2,431,763	1,307,772	103,642
1984	2,031,416	2,285,926	2,540,656	1,275,410	107,571
1985	2,423,844	2,798,396	3,186,030	1,537,926	111,819
1986	2,804,143	3,322,187	3,874,394	1,684,485	116,066
1987	2,918,984	3,532,466	4,199,865	1,649,118	117,340
1988	3,185,537	3,956,611	4,816,478	1,783,181	122,544
1989	3,565,683	4,509,400	5,575,498	2,176,464	127,960
1990	3,418,203	4,261,938	5,179,053	1,977,755	133,906
1991	3,928,704	5,002,214	6,190,194	2,396,460	142,083
1992	3,993,855	5,117,479	6,355,536	2,422,605	146,437
1993	4,494,698	5,911,715	7,511,973	2,498,881	150,684
1994	4,290,550	5,731,646	7,374,395	2,374,699	154,826
1995	4,788,996	6,465,844	8,377,790	3,045,069	158,967
1996	4,948,978	6,816,309	8,977,556	3,547,080	163,002
1997	5,078,357	7,058,243	9,345,375	4,505,993	168,418
1998	5,212,608	7,295,846	9,689,625	5,573,536	171,285
1999	5,434,063	7,848,682	10,708,876	6,535,151	174,046
2000	5,566,795	8,023,518	10,872,987	5,778,238	178,719
2001	5,590,261	8,076,720	10,919,406	4,928,813	184,771
2002	5,638,423	8,074,884	10,764,532	3,693,084	187,639
2003	6,606,964	9,927,928	13,801,225	4,505,443	192,099
2004	7,178,789	11,106,557	15,810,741	4,778,320	195,709

	40% Global Equity	50% Global Equity	60% Global Equity	S&P 500 Index W/Divs	Distributions
2005	7,423,116	11,742,968	17,002,591	4,800,560	202,080
2006	8,040,096	13,115,813	19,469,586	5,317,291	208,983
2007	8,333,958	13,660,796	20,265,346	5,383,357	214,292
2008	7,150,390	11,191,823	15,711,835	3,251,153	223,038
2009	8,044,167	13,136,750	19,105,807	3,829,207	223,242
2010	8,708,855	14,590,382	21,633,261	4,142,045	229,317

*See text for explanation. Data copyright © 2011 Merriman, Inc.

As you'll see, every one of these portfolios survived in good shape all the way through 2010. Further, the total period here, 41 years, is longer than most people expect to live after retiring.

Variable or Flexible Distributions

For a long time I have believed that one of life's ultimate financial luxuries is to have saved enough money to take flexible distributions in retirement. Now I'd like to show you in two other tables why I think that is a luxury.

A flexible distribution is one that goes up and down from year to year, not based on inflation but according to the value of your portfolio. In other words, it automatically does what most smart retirees would naturally want to do if they could—take out more money after good years and scale back on withdrawals when their investments are suffering.

This is very nice when investment returns are good. But it can be pretty uncomfortable in bad times. Recall for a moment the first five years in the first table. The retiree on fixed distributions took out more money every year regardless of what the stock market was doing. Those withdrawals were insulated from that big bad bear market of 1973 and 1974—but they took a heavy toll on portfolios.

The following table shows a flexible distribution plan that also started out with an aggressive $60,000 withdrawal in 1970. The layout of this table is different from that of the first two. In this flexible plan, every year's distribution was different for each portfolio allocation.

AGGRESSIVE FLEXIBLE DISTRIBUTION SCHEDULE*

	60% Global Equity/40% Bonds			S&P 500 Index W/Divs		
	Year-End Balance	Distribution	Cumulative Distribution	Year-End Balance	Distribution	Cumulative Distribution
1970	964,684	60,000	60,000	977,845	60,000	60,000
1971	1,087,376	57,881	117,881	1,050,781	58,671	118,671
1972	1,203,425	65,243	183,124	1,175,165	63,047	181,718
1973	1,018,578	72,206	255,329	942,647	70,510	252,227
1974	839,214	61,115	316,444	651,645	56,559	308,786
1975	1,025,729	50,353	366,797	840,486	39,099	347,885
1976	1,128,828	61,544	428,340	978,478	50,429	398,314
1977	1,238,732	67,730	496,070	853,736	58,709	457,023
1978	1,385,448	74,324	570,394	855,269	51,224	508,247
1979	1,438,889	83,127	653,521	952,072	51,316	559,563
1980	1,600,480	86,333	739,854	1,184,980	57,124	616,687
1981	1,575,534	96,029	835,883	1,059,203	71,099	687,786
1982	1,730,451	94,532	930,415	1,208,814	63,552	751,338
1983	1,971,901	103,827	1,034,242	1,392,106	72,529	823,867
1984	2,023,711	118,314	1,152,556	1,390,580	83,526	907,394
1985	2,492,165	121,423	1,273,979	1,727,662	83,435	990,828
1986	2,952,834	149,530	1,423,509	1,923,964	103,660	1,094,488
1987	3,099,362	177,170	1,600,679	1,903,126	115,438	1,209,926
1988	3,437,431	185,962	1,786,640	2,089,646	114,188	1,324,113
1989	3,838,021	206,246	1,992,886	2,582,832	125,379	1,449,492
1990	3,429,875	230,281	2,223,168	2,350,834	154,970	1,604,462
1991	3,957,142	205,793	2,428,960	2,884,861	141,050	1,745,512
1992	3,906,797	237,429	2,666,389	2,919,768	173,092	1,918,604
1993	4,440,304	234,408	2,900,796	3,018,760	175,186	2,093,790
1994	4,178,464	266,418	3,167,215	2,874,731	181,126	2,274,916
1995	4,554,154	250,708	3,417,922	3,713,685	172,484	2,447,399
1996	4,672,167	273,249	3,691,172	4,296,353	222,821	2,670,221
1997	4,652,804	280,330	3,971,502	5,386,089	257,781	2,928,002
1998	4,612,838	279,168	4,250,670	6,509,870	323,165	3,251,167
1999	4,872,701	276,770	4,527,440	7,406,331	390,592	3,641,759

	60% Global Equity/40% Bonds			S&P 500 Index W/Divs		
	Year-End Balance	Distribution	Cumulative Distribution	Year-End Balance	Distribution	Cumulative Distribution
2000	4,722,801	292,362	4,819,802	6,328,678	444,380	4,086,139
2001	4,528,850	283,368	5,103,170	5,242,062	379,721	4,465,860
2002	4,263,436	271,731	5,374,901	3,838,250	314,524	4,780,384
2003	5,222,430	255,806	5,630,708	4,643,103	230,295	5,010,679
2004	5,697,721	313,346	5,944,053	4,839,059	278,586	5,289,265
2005	5,827,841	341,863	6,285,917	4,771,686	290,344	5,579,608
2006	6,344,644	349,670	6,635,587	5,194,315	286,301	5,865,909
2007	6,271,388	380,679	7,016,266	5,150,909	311,659	6,177,568
2008	4,617,243	376,283	7,392,549	3,050,511	309,055	6,486,623
2009	5,345,681	277,035	7,669,584	3,626,321	183,031	6,669,653
2010	5,751,876	320,741	7,990,324	3,922,109	217,579	6,887,233

*See text for explanation. Data copyright © 2011 Merriman, Inc.

Now here is a variation of the same table, this time showing withdrawals taken at a more conservative rate.

CONSERVATIVE FLEXIBLE DISTRIBUTION SCHEDULE*

	60% Global Equity/40% Bonds			S&P 500 Index W/Divs		
	Year-End Balance	Distribution	Cumulative Distribution	Year-End Balance	Distribution	Cumulative Distribution
1970	985,447	40,000	40,000	998,650	40,000	40,000
1971	1,134,690	39,418	79,418	1,095,970	39,946	79,946
1972	1,283,515	45,388	124,805	1,251,783	43,839	123,785
1973	1,109,724	51,341	176,146	1,025,469	50,071	173,856
1974	934,498	44,389	220,535	723,982	41,019	214,875
1975	1,166,894	37,380	257,915	953,654	28,959	243,834
1976	1,312,536	46,676	304,591	1,133,847	38,146	281,980
1977	1,472,540	52,501	357,092	1,010,347	45,354	327,334
1978	1,683,556	58,902	415,994	1,033,696	40,414	367,748
1979	1,787,617	67,342	483,336	1,175,178	41,348	409,096
1980	2,032,622	71,505	554,841	1,493,785	47,007	456,103

continued

CONSERVATIVE FLEXIBLE DISTRIBUTION SCHEDULE* (CONTINUED)

	60% Global Equity/40% Bonds			S&P 500 Index W/Divs		
	Year-End Balance	Distribution	Cumulative Distribution	Year-End Balance	Distribution	Cumulative Distribution
1981	2,045,434	81,305	636,146	1,363,640	59,751	515,855
1982	2,297,094	81,817	717,963	1,589,364	54,546	570,400
1983	2,676,579	91,884	809,847	1,869,303	63,575	633,975
1984	2,809,929	107,063	916,910	1,906,982	74,772	708,747
1985	3,540,296	112,397	1,029,307	2,419,652	76,279	785,026
1986	4,290,920	141,612	1,170,919	2,751,911	96,786	881,812
1987	4,605,817	171,637	1,342,556	2,780,023	110,076	991,889
1988	5,224,382	184,233	1,526,788	3,117,432	111,201	1,103,090
1989	5,964,880	208,975	1,735,764	3,935,172	124,697	1,227,787
1990	5,450,337	238,595	1,974,359	3,657,909	157,407	1,385,194
1991	6,430,650	218,013	2,192,372	4,584,366	146,316	1,531,510
1992	6,491,954	257,226	2,449,598	4,738,557	183,375	1,714,885
1993	7,544,818	259,678	2,709,276	5,003,452	189,542	1,904,427
1994	7,259,400	301,793	3,011,069	4,866,107	200,138	2,104,565
1995	8,090,873	290,376	3,301,445	6,419,970	194,644	2,299,209
1996	8,487,298	323,635	3,625,080	7,585,272	256,799	2,556,008
1997	8,642,397	339,492	3,964,572	9,711,541	303,411	2,859,419
1998	8,761,317	345,696	4,310,268	11,987,547	388,462	3,247,881
1999	9,463,662	350,453	4,660,721	13,928,504	479,502	3,727,383
2000	9,379,377	378,546	5,039,267	12,155,078	557,140	4,284,523
2001	9,197,368	375,175	5,414,442	10,282,300	486,203	4,770,726
2002	8,854,664	367,895	5,782,337	7,688,910	411,292	5,182,018
2003	11,093,849	354,187	6,136,523	9,499,116	307,556	5,489,574
2004	12,375,053	443,754	6,580,277	10,110,652	379,965	5,869,539
2005	12,939,630	495,002	7,075,279	10,182,010	404,426	6,273,965
2006	14,399,886	517,585	7,592,865	11,319,658	407,280	6,681,245
2007	14,547,398	575,995	8,168,860	11,463,898	452,786	7,134,032
2008	10,946,793	581,896	8,750,756	6,933,690	458,556	7,592,588
2009	12,961,880	437,872	9,188,628	8,417,854	277,348	7,869,935
2010	14,259,122	518,475	9,707,103	9,298,186	336,714	8,206,649

*See text for explanation. Data copyright © 2011 Merriman, Inc.

You can see that in both the portfolios we show, distributions fell quickly, reflecting the stock market. In the aggressive flexible 60 percent equity portfolio, the annual distribution fell to $50,353 in 1975. If you really needed $60,000 to cover your cost of living, that had to hurt. This flexible distribution regained its $60,000 level the following year, but at the start of 1975, there was no way to know that would happen.

You can see that in 1975, the distribution in each column was at its low point, reflecting the stock market's dismal performance in the previous two years. From there distributions went up.

It's interesting to compare the growth of distributions over the years in the fixed and flexible distribution plans. Eventually, the flexible plans provided more money than the fixed ones. But in the 2nd through 17th years of retirement, retirees in the flexible plan had to make do with less purchasing power than they had in 1970.

Is that really an "ultimate luxury"? You may be wondering why anybody would be willing to embark on a flexible plan like this. It's a very good question. I think it's a luxury only if you have saved more money than you really need.

For example, imagine you retired with investments worth $1.5 million instead of the $1 million shown in these tables and that you needed $60,000 to meet your desired cost of living. In this case, you could start by taking out $90,000, giving yourself quite a cushion that first year. To see how that would have played out, multiply every distribution by 1.5.

In the table, the 60 percent equity portfolio's distribution reaches a low of $50,353 in 1975. But if you were taking out 1.5 times the amounts shown, you would have had about $75,500, which would have been still well above your "needs," even accounting for inflation.

In this scenario, from the first day of your retirement you will have extra money for whatever you want to do. That's a luxury, as long as you don't build that extra money into your lifestyle so you must have it.

Letting this play out with the numbers in the aggressive flexible distribution table, in your 11th year of retirement, in 1980, you would have withdrawn nearly $130,000, 1.5 times the figure shown in the table. From that point forward, your flexible distributions would have continued to rise nicely.

At least as important, your portfolio would have easily survived for 41 years, longer than most retirees are likely to live. Remember, this seemingly abundant retirement was possible because you had saved 1.5 times as much as you really needed.

Fixed Versus Variable Withdrawal Rate

Here's my take on fixed versus variable. If you have saved more than enough money to meet your needs with an inflation-adjusted "fixed" withdrawal rate, you may be able to afford the sort of flexible distribution plan shown in the last two tables. Your income then will be determined by your investment results instead of by inflation.

During the years in this study, this would have given you more spending power and more to leave to your heirs. However, these results are highly dependent on the unpredictable returns of the stock market and (to a smaller degree) the bond market.

Therefore my advice is simple: Save more than you think you will ever need. I will be pretty surprised if I ever get an e-mail from you complaining that your life is miserable because you have saved too much money.

Take Out More? Take Out Less?

There is nothing cast in stone about taking 4 percent or 6 percent from a retirement portfolio every year. After the market meltdown of 2007 and 2008, financial planners and advisors increasingly favor 4 percent as prudent and conservative. You can see hypothetical results in the tables in this appendix. In general, a portfolio is likely to last longer if you take out less. For people who retire early, that's an extremely important consideration.

People with relatively short life expectancies and no burning desire to leave money to their heirs can take out more. Those who care about what they leave to posterity may be satisfied to live on less. This is a balancing act.

Lessons from These Numbers

If this discussion leaves you with only one lesson, I hope it is the value of having more money, instead of less, when you retire.

Of course we don't always have a choice about when we retire. In those cases our resources are whatever they are, and our challenge becomes finding ways to make the most of them. These tables will help you think about how to do that, based on your own circumstances.

One simple way for many people to improve their financial outlook in retirement is to work a few extra years.

This has at least four important benefits:

1. Additional years on the job will let you add more to your savings.

2. Your portfolio will have more time to potentially grow before it must start paying you. I have seen cases in which these first two benefits combined to boost the value of a portfolio by 50 percent in five extra years of working.

3. Retiring later means your portfolio will have fewer years it must pay you, so those payouts can be larger.

4. If you delay taking Social Security, your payments will be permanently higher.

Finally, if you are a young person with many years before you plan to retire, I hope you will consider ramping up your savings plan, now that you know more about how retirement income really works.

What I've shown here is not a definitive set of final solutions. In an ideal world, you could adopt a plan on the first day of your retirement and mechanically follow it the rest of your life. But real life is rarely that simple. Use these tables and this discussion to guide your thinking. If you have a financial advisor, make sure he or she helps you figure this out.

If you can find a withdrawal plan that does a good job of dealing with your resources, your needs, and your wants, then you have found the sleep-easy plan that's right for you. I hope you will find it.

APPENDIX I
Hiring an Investment Advisor

One of the smartest things investors can do is hire the right professional help to get them on track and keep them there. In this appendix, I tell why that matters and how to find good help.

Throughout this book I have mentioned the benefits of getting professional help with your investments. I am biased on this point by the fact that I founded an investment advisory firm, and you will have to consider that as you evaluate what you read here.

If you absorb what's in this book and apply it as I have suggested in Chapter 10, "Twelve Numbers to Change Your Life," then in theory you can do everything you need without professional help. However, I don't do that, and I'd like to tell you why.

I know my way around the investment world pretty well, and still I have an advisor on whom I rely. He helps me keep my perspective. Sometimes he tells me to do things that I don't want to do, such as spend more of my money. Sometimes he does necessary chores that I don't want to do, such as rebalancing my portfolio.

It's true that the help of an investment advisor will cost you money. But I have seen over and over again that a well-chosen advisor, used appropriately, is likely to be worth many times the fee you will pay for this help.

You may be very good at doing many things. You may be a quick learner and rarely if ever repeat a mistake. But finance is complex, and Wall Street has an overwhelming desire to make money from you. The odds are not in your favor.

Many investors have told me over the years that they "will know" when it's time to get in or get out, that they "will know" what stocks to buy or which mutual fund managers to trust. And yet I've heard at least as many investors say they've been stunned by what happened to the markets and to their portfolios.

Global markets react instantly to all sorts of things. Even if you're listening to the financial news constantly, by the time you learn some important fact, professional traders will have already responded. If the news contains some huge opportunity, they will have taken it before you find out. If there's a huge new peril, the professionals will protect themselves before you get a chance to even think about it.

You may think you know enough to make smart, informed decisions. But you probably don't have time to learn everything you need to know.

It takes years to become a certified financial planner (C.F.P.), and with good reason. When you are responsible for somebody else's money, there's a lot you have to know. In addition, you had better be aware of a lot of other things—even if you're not expert in them—that could affect your clients.

If you are serious about being a successful investor, the right professional advisor can do at least three very important things for you.

First, your advisor can help you get clarity about what you need to do. There are thousands of opportunities to invest your money, and a clever sales pitch is waiting behind every one. Charting your course requires thinking about a lot of things including taxes, inflation, and risk. Once you figure out where you need to go, you need a plan. You'll almost certainly have a better plan if you get a professional to help you create it than if you do it yourself.

Second, your advisor can help you find the best way to implement your plan and your strategy as well as help you exercise the discipline to carry it out. In my view, this last piece is valuable enough to tip the scale even if you get nothing else.

Third, ideally your advisor can help you with noninvestment financial decisions that may involve insurance, doing estate planning, refinancing your mortgage, exercising stock options, loaning money to family members, and even making business decisions. I'm not suggesting you are likely to find an advisor who is an expert in all those fields. But a good advisor can point you in the right directions, be a neutral sounding board, and direct you to the experts who can help the most.

So let's turn to a very practical question. Where can you find the best advisor?

Finding the Best Advisor

This is a big topic, and entire books have been written about it. But it doesn't take long to cover the most important points. I can sum it up very simply this way: The most important qualities to look for are competence and ethics.

A winning personality is nice. So is somebody who golfs with your friends, who belongs to the same club, or whose daughter goes to school with your daughter. But what you really want is a combination of competence and ethics. This has nothing to do with friendship.

First, you should have an advisor who is on your side—someone who has a fiduciary duty to you. *Fiduciary* is a big, formal word with a specific legal meaning—someone who is required by law to do what is best for you and to put your interests ahead of his or her own. No conflicts of interest, in other words. You'll be most likely to find this when you work with someone whose compensation comes from you, not from the companies that make financial products.

Second, you should have an advisor who is educated, knowledgeable, and experienced. Anybody who has the C.F.P. credential has passed multiple rigorous tests of knowledge and has at least a few years of practical experience working with clients. If you don't need a specialist in some specific area such as taxation, law, or securities analysis, I think a C.F.P. is likely to have enough broad exposure to the world of money to act as a generalist. In most cases, I think that is what you want.

Third, your advisor should be someone you trust enough to confide in, whose advice and counsel you will follow—even when you may not feel like it. You may have an advisor with all the credentials in the world, but if the personality match is bad, or if you don't totally trust the person, you have the wrong advisor.

Fourth (and this is something you don't read about very much), I think you should have an advisor who is age-appropriate for you. When you are young, say in your 20s and 30s, I think you'll do best with an advisor who is older than you, somebody who can bring years if not decades of personal experience and perspective to the table for your benefit. These are your learning years, and you should be the one doing the learning.

When you are nearing retirement or already retired, you want somebody who's younger than you are, somebody who's likely to be in the business for the rest of your life.

Finally, let's get even more specific.

If you want somebody to manage your money on a continuing basis, I recommend finding an advisor who uses Dimensional Fund Advisors funds. Dimensional Fund Advisors won't let just anybody use its funds for clients. Many advisory firms have passed Dimensional's screening, and this is to your benefit. You can find them easily if you start at the company's website, http://www.dfaus.com/.

If you are looking for help on an hourly basis, I recommend somebody who has the credentials of a C.F.P. As I mentioned, anybody who qualifies for that designation has a good grasp of investments, taxes, insurance, retirement planning, and other financial matters. If you are—or if you expect to be—in a high tax bracket, see if you can find a C.F.P. who is also a certified public accountant (C.P.A.).

One other worthwhile combination is a C.P.A. who has earned the additional designation of Personal Finance Specialist.

You may have to interview several people to find someone who is the right match for you. But if you are successful, you will have a partner who can help you find lots of ways to stay financially fit forever.

INDEX

ABOUT THE AUTHORS

Paul Merriman is nationally recognized as an authority on mutual funds, index investing, buy-and-hold and active investment strategies, and asset allocation. He is the founder of Paul A. Merriman and Associates, an investment advisory firm devoted to helping all investors successfully navigate through the ups and downs of market cycles. The company has evolved into Merriman Inc., employing a staff of 40 and managing $1.5 billion for more than two thousand households throughout the United States.

Paul is the author of four books on personal investing. His most recent, *Live It Up Without Outliving Your Money!* (Wiley, 2008), has been among the leading personal finance books sold at Amazon.com (http://www.amazon.com/).

He has led hundreds of workshops for investors, hosted a weekly radio program, and been a frequent featured guest on national television shows. *Forbes* named FundAdvice.com (http://www.fundad vice.com/), published by Merriman Inc., one of the best investment resources on the Internet. His weekly podcast, "Sound Investing," was named by *Money Magazine* as "the best money podcast." Paul is widely quoted in many national publications and is frequently invited to speak before local chapters of the American Association of Individual Investors. He has twice been the featured guest speaker at Harvard University's investor psychology conference.

Prior to founding Paul A. Merriman and Associates, he briefly worked as a broker for a major Wall Street firm in the mid-1960s. Recognizing that Wall Street was fraught with too many conflicts of interest, he decided to help small companies raise venture capital. Then, in 1979, he became president and chairman of a public manufacturing company in the Pacific Northwest. He retired in 1982 to create his investment management firm.

Paul is the recipient of a distinguished alumni award from Western Washington University's School of Economics and a founding member of the board of directors of Global HELP.

Richard Buck began subscribing to investment newsletters when he was in high school, and he has never lost his fascination with all the ways that money can be put to work. After receiving a bachelor's degree in history from Willamette University, he began a 30-year career as a journalist, including eight years as a writer and editor at the Associated Press and 20 years as a business reporter for *The Seattle Times.*

In 1993, he became a ghostwriter for two newsletters published by Paul Merriman's advisory company. Four years later he was hired by Paul as publications manager. In that role he has written hundreds of articles on various aspects of investing. He was the ghostwriter for Paul's most recent book, *Live It Up Without Outliving Your Money!*

His writing has been published in travel magazines, outdoor magazines, and in "America," a publication of the U.S. State Department.

In his spare time he has been chairman of the board of a Seattle credit union, co-founder of an international exchange program, president of the Willamette University Alumni Association, and a member of the university's board of trustees.